City Manager:
Roddy Allen

Sales & Marketing:
Corrie Mills, Campbell Deeming

Design:
Matt Wood, Chris McNamara

Photography:
Ben Wicks
Generic people shots © Matt Smith*

Team itchy:
Lisa Ellwood, John Emmerson, Sharon Evans, Si Gray
Emma Howarth, Ruby Quince, Si Smith, Emma Tilley,
Mike Waugh,Kim Whatley, Andrew Wood

Contributors:
Scott Baker-Marflitt, Richard Biggs, Karl Bryne, Susan Casey, Neil Chue Hong,
Barbara De Moubray, Mark Evans, Sharon Gibb, Beatie Hitchman,
Whitney Kassel, Lissi Maimaris, Corrie Mills, Lola Okolosie, Nichola Osborne,
Steph Page, Lyndsey Purvis, Hannah Summers, Steph Wright, Bulent Yusef

Acknowledgments:
Laurie Pegg and Bill Walsh

* Contact on 07779 134984

Globe Quay, Globe Road, Leeds LS11 5QG
t: 0113 246 0440 f: 0113 246 0550

Black Bull Yard, 24-28 Hatton Wall, London EC1N 8JH
t: 020 7405 9905 f: 020 7404 4533
e: all@itchymedia.co.uk www.itchycity.co.uk

ISBN: 1-903753-35-X

Get out more

The all-new Ford**Fiesta**

Designed for living
engineered to last

contents

www.itchycity.co.uk

Take a few million tourists, a proper party atmosphere, some impressive architecture, a load of posh students, more culture than you can shake a stick at, and one hell of a lot of festival mayhem and you'll find yourself somewhere in the vicinity of Edinburgh.

Scotland's first city has plenty to offer your average visitor – whether you're here for the weekend or thinking about staying for a lifetime. And for those of us who already call Edinburgh home, there's more than enough new bars, clubs, restaurants, shops and the like opening each year to keep us in pints and fancy sushi for eternity. For your annual update of all that's happening in the city, tchy Edinburgh is on the case, for the highs, the lows and the in betweens.

You'll find all the usual reviews and recommendations, fully updated and as opinionated as ever. We've also constructed some ridiculously sensible and organised Useful Info tables so you'll never be stuck without a cab number/hotel/kebab at 4am ever again, and for the second year running our Laters section should sort you out for the darker side of life. So basically, whether you're after somewhere to take your gran out for lunch or some quality hip hop for a big night out, you're in safe hands.

For those of you who wish to venture outside of the main drag, if only to avoid tourists asking you where the nearest McDonald's/Starbucks/man in a kilt is then we've devised a little section to show you how, imaginatively titled Out of Areas.

Mingle with the locals, get down with the tourists, schmooze the festival thespians and try to ignore what seems like every Hogmanay-celebrating Australian backpacker in the entire UK. Get stuck into what is, in our opinion (which quite frankly is all you're going to get here) one hell of a fine city.

Edinburgh, we salute you.

○ Two hours in Edinburgh

Right, you're in a hurry so we'll be brief. With limited time you might as well stay north of Princes Street and check out what the 'sophisticated' side of town has to offer. First stop **Jenner's** (the so-called Harrod's of the North) for a quick spot of shopping – don't bother heading further down Princes Street – you'll only find what you can see on any other shopping street in Britain. If it's culture you're after then nip over the road and trundle around **The National Gallery of Scotland**. Recharge in **Oloroso**, the newest place on George Street, from their roof terrace you'll be able to see right across Edinburgh and all that you've missed. For those of you hanging around past sundown, nip round to **Tonic**, catching a glimpse of the **Castle** on your way, and knock back a cocktail from their hangover inducing range, or head round to **La Tasca** for a little sangria and tapas with your drinks. And after all that you'll have forgotten why you had to leave and probably want to stay for at least another...

○ Two days in Edinburgh

Packed full of tourist delights and with enough bars and restaurants to keep you pickled and stuffed for a life time, Edinburgh deserves more than a puny little weekend trip, but you only have two days so we'll have to keep it brief...

Stay – at the **Point Hotel** for its centrality and funky décor or, if you prefer to stick with a name you know, Edinburgh's **Malmaison** in Leith is recommended.

Shop – on **George Street** for all the big designer names or head to **Victoria Street** for some of Edinburgh's more unusual shops. For edible gifts, head down to Leith to Scotland's oldest deli, **Valvona & Crolla**, and whilst you're there you might as well try the café too.

Attractions – for some hardcore tourist action hit the **Royal Mile** and head up to the **Castle** for a quick tour. Fit in a bit of culture whilst you're here, the **Dean Gallery** and the **Modern Art Gallery** are worth a look.

Eat – for the ultimate in posh cuisine try **The Witchery**, **David Bann** or the **Tower** in the impressive **Museum of Scotland** building. For quality seafood try the recently refurbished **Creelers** restaurant. Slightly south of the centre, **The Apartment** is worth a detour.

Drink – **Beluga**, **Monboddo** and **Opal Lounge** are all a good bet if cocktails are your thing. **EH1** on the Royal Mile is a great pre-club drinking venue. Alternatively, for a chilled out bevvie nip over to Broughton Street and try **Basement**, **Outhouse** or newcomer **Mezz**.

Club – try **Beat Club** for live jazz until the wee small hours. Or, if you're up for something a little bit more high energy, **Ego** is worth a look. Finally, if you don't mind your clubbing scruffy, **Bongo Club** is home to some of Edinburgh's best alternative nights.

O Two days on the cheap

Edinburgh likes to think of herself as that little bit posher than her sister, Glasgow, and she is certainly a wee bit more costly. Never fear we good people at itchy are here to help you poorer folk out...

Stay – at one of Edinburgh's many hostels, the only place you'll find for less are the park benches in Princes Street Gardens. Try **Backpacker's Hostel**. (Cost: £22)

Shop – on **Cockburn Street** for some interesting window shopping and to pick up some bargain music at **Fopp** (Cost: £10 for a couple of classic CDs). If you're looking for clothes on the cheap, then pop into **Armstrongs** or **YoYo** for some vintage fashion. (Cost: £20)

Attractions – Edinburgh's nae cheap so you'll need to stick to the city's toll free sights. First choice is **Arthur's seat**, or its smaller neighbour **Calton Hill**, for some cracking views of Auld Reekie. Edinburgh's free art galleries are worth a look; try the

Stills and the **Fruitmarket** for some contemporary exhibits. During the Festival wander along the **Royal Mile** and check out the abundance of street performers vying for attention. (Cost: £1 tip for the fire-eater)

Eat – Cheap tucker is not Edinburgh's speciality, but it's worth checking cheaper lunch time deals and filling up for the day. **Yo!Below** is a fantastically kitsch night out with Sushi, karaoke and gimmicks-a-plenty at damned reasonable prices (£6.95 a bowl of noodles). 'Whose Lunch is it Anyway' every Sunday 1pm at **The Stand** offers a tasty lunch for a mere £4 and free improvised comedy for hangover relief. (Cost: £10)

Drink – The best way to pick up a cheap drink is to keep an eye out for happy hours. Try **Three Sisters**, **Living Room** and **Indigo Yard** at the weekend for some of the best offers. (Cost: £20 see how long you can make it last)

Club – **Berlin Bierhaus** is free until three, the beer may a bit more expensive but it's top-notch premium quality. You'll also get free entry into **Espionage** (although you may regret it once you're in there). (Cost: £25 knock back a few foreign lagers)

Total: £100

itchy feat #47

This year, the itchy reviews are **72%** gobbledegook. **33%** have been made up... **31%** are a good guess and **8%** don't even exist. *

Tell the world what you think of your **favourite** bar and **hated** club by adding your comments

Vent your spleen @ www.itchycity.co.uk

*might be, might not be... you tell me

○ Duddingston

Tucked at the bottom of Arthur's Seat, a visit to Duddingston village is like gate crashing the set of the Beeb's latest costume drama.

Proper Boozer
Sheep's Heid Inn
43-45 The Causeway (0131)656 6957
Scotland's oldest licensed pub with added bonus of old style bowling alley at £10p/h.

○ Leith

Famous as Trainspotting territory, Leith is starting to look like the trendy end of town.

Good Eats
Valvona & Crolla
19 Elm Row (0131) 556 6066
Scotland's oldest deli is a treasure trove of Italian goodies and also boasts an extravagant café. *Mon-Sat 8pm-6pm*

Food OnThe Go
The Globe
23 Bernard Street (0131) 625 5552

Not To Be Missed
The sunshine on Leith

○ Marchmont

Student central, but Marchmont becomes a ghost town out of term time.

Proper Boozer
The Earl of Marchmont
22 Marchmont Crescent (0131) 667 1398
Think Lou's Place in Neighbours.

Hangover Breakfast
Caffe Politik
146-148 Marchmont Rd (0131) 446 9873
Healthy portions and crusty bread. Lenin would approve.

Not To Be Missed
Oak Leaf Co.
4 Roseneath Street (0131) 229 9933
Crammed full of complimentary therapies so you needn't spend a penny.

Also Not To Be Missed
The Meadows (in Summer)
Juggling, sunbathing, footie & illegal BBQs.

○ Stockbridge

The young professional part of town is proof that 9-5ers know how to have a good time.

Proper Boozer
Baillie
2-4 St Stephen Street (0131) 225 9397
Lively pub for all ages (over 18 that is). Check out the authentic 70s pictures on the walls of St Stephen's Street hippies. Look carefully and you might find your mum and dad.

Cheap Meal
33a JM's French Bistro
St Stephen Street (0131) 225 9397
Cordon-bleu cuisine and BYO wine in a tiny Stockbridge basement.

Not To Be Missed
Floatarium
29 North West Circus Pl (0131) 225 3350
Absolute bliss. Forget about your troubles and feel your stress slip away.

the do's and don'ts of Edinburgh life...

Sam, 24, Assistant manager of Victoria and Albert

I'm a Home Counties girl who's fallen in love with Edinburgh. I like to drink in the Grassmarket area, but when it comes to fins it has to be the Victoria and Albert of course! The city is so friendly and there's loads to keep you entertained. I can't stand the pretentious guys in suits who frequent the city's bars or Leith Docks because they look ugly, but besides that this is the best city in the UK.

Michael, 21, Iguana Barman

I've only been in Edinburgh for a year, but the nightlife is outstanding, really trendy with loads of places to go. The weather's shite, but I'm from Belfast so I'm used to that. My favourite bar is the Opal Lounge, and I get all my threads from Xile in Princess Mall when I can afford to. I usually head to the Peppermint Lounge for my clubbing fix, but I'm always too pissed to remember why!

AJ, 23, Student

I'm from London, but I much prefer it here as it's quieter, more peaceful and full of friendly people. I can't even think of a worst thing about the place as I've not seen one yet. Bar Kohl is my favourite bar. I also like the Wok Bar where I indulge in as many hot 'n' spicy dishes as possible. I'm still finding new places all the time so come and ask me next year when I'll know a lot more...

Laura, 23, Urban Design Student

I've just been to Beluga which is a visually stunning bar. I'm a bit worse for wear so I can't say too much but the old town is the best part of the city because it's so pretty, but we need more trams and trains to go out into the burbs, especially at four in the morning.

Rachel and Naomi, Art students

Being art students we like to visit the Doggerfisher Gallery between Broughton and Leith, or the Talbot Gallery for inspiration. For a bite to eat we keep returning to the African Café where they do some great middle eastern platters, and Kalpna does some of the best veggie food in town. We both enjoy a bit of jazz so Henry's is a favourite, although the Bongo Club is a classic with their selection of reggae, dub and world music with a bit of poetry thrown in. The best thing about Edinburgh is the festivals. Worst thing has to be the pain in the legs from all the hills.

Frank, 43, Artist

This is a hugely inspiring place to work as an artist. You have a variety of architecture, unlike a lot of cities which are associated with one style. I can't get enough of the place, and won't say a bad word against it. Nexus is ideal for coffee and East End on Broughton Street does me for food. I don't bother much with clothes as I only end up getting paint on them.

Craig, 30, Culinary Connoisseur

The best thing about this place is that the pubs never shut. I'm from England and it's a real treat not to have to leave the boozer at ten past eleven. The worst thing is all the bloody English – like me! I enjoy a drink in Isobar because all the Schemies walk right past as it's too chilled for them. The Phoenix cellar bar on Broughton Street is where you'll always find me on the last Sunday of the month when it's cheesy tunes all the way. I usually treat myself to a Burger King after-wards, I like to live it up me.

Mark, 26, Barman

When I'm not serving up drinks I'll usually be around Broughton Street – take your pick, there's so many great bars to go to. When it comes to clubs then the cheesier the better such as CC Blooms. You can't beat Blue Moon Café for food, I know I work there, but it's true. The gay triangle is the best thing about Edinburgh for me, it's so much more chilled than Soho. The weather is the worst thing – they should look at towing Scotland to the Caribbean.

restaurants
www.itchyedinburgh.co.uk

○ American

Buffalo Grill
12-14 Chapel Street (0131) 667 7427
1 Raeburn Place (0131) 332 3864

Most steakhouses deal only in prime cuts of cow, but the well-established Buffalo Grill makes some fantastic detours into poultry, seafood and vegetarian food. It has to be said that it's the beef that shines through but if you find yourself here without an urge to get some meat inside you, the rest of the menu is well worth a look. Check out some of the more interesting options like The Carpetbag (prime steak with grilled oysters) and get into the relaxed vibe.

Chapel Street: Mon-Fri 12pm-2pm, 6pm-10.15pm, Sat 6pm-10.15pm, Sun 5pm-10pm
Raeburn Place: Mon-Thu 12pm-2.30pm, 6pm-10.30pm, Fri 12pm-2.30pm, 6pm-11pm, Sat 11am-4pm, 5pm-11pm, Sun 11am-4pm, 5pm-10.30pm
Recommended dish: Carpetbag steak £14.95. House wine: £7.95 (Raeburn Place only). BYO at both venues

Way Out →

The all-new Ford**Fiesta**

Designed for living
engineered to last

Filling Station
235 High Street (0131) 226 2488

Bog standard Tex-Mex restaurant rife with tourists proclaiming the sizes of the portions too small compared to those in their beloved America (don't listen to them, we still reckon they're pretty massive). The décor's your standard tacky array of Americana and dodgy memorabilia, the staff have irritating perma grins and the noise levels escalate to insane levels as the night goes on. Take sedatives, drink yourself into a stupor or take our advice and just don't bother. This place is truly lame, and we've seen some lame places in our time.
Mon-Sat 12pm-11.30pm, Sun 12.30pm-10.30pm (bar open 11.30am-12am, 1am at weekends). Rec. dish: Burgers £6.85-£7.75. House wine: £10.50

ⓘ Recommended
Cheap Eats
- Flaming Red Dining Room
- Made in Italy
- Mama's
- Standing Order
- Wok Bar (lunch time) ⓘ

Frankie & Benny's
Kinnaird Park (0131) 657 2766

I know what I fancy doing tonight. I'd like to go to a restaurant in a shopping centre that shuts stupidly early and serves incredibly average food to a selection of idiots that frankly must be too drunk or stupid to know better. I'd like to hang out with hens, stags and an army of screaming kids. I am most at

home in the midst of total and utter mediocrity. Look, basically, eat here if you really must, but please don't say we sent you.
Mon-Thu 11am-9pm, Fri-Sun 11am-10pm Rec. dish: Barbecue chicken and ribs £9.95. House wine: £8.45

Garfunkel's
29-31 Frederick Street (0131) 225 4579

It may be another (yes, another) city centre chain but at least Garfunkel's have a good attitude and a speciality. The speciality is the killer ice-cream based desserts which are worth a visit on their own never mind the rest of the menu. The staff are saintly and able to handle whatever the customers throw at them and the atmosphere is surprisingly calm.
Sun-Thu 12pm-12am, Fri-Sat 12pm-1am Rec. dish: Salad bar £6.50. House wine: £10

Hard Rock Café
30 George Street (0131) 260 3000

It's brash, noisy and OTT, but they certainly know how to cook a burger. Probably not your first choice for a bite to eat, but if you can cope with the stimulus overload, and the inevitable kids' party, the original themed restaurant may be for you, especially if you're hungry. At first glance everything seems overpriced, but once you tuck into the huge portions laid before you, you realise that it's worth every cent. Three courses may seem impossible, but the bubbly staff are always on hand to recommend their favourite if you can fit it in. *Mon-Thu 12pm-11pm, Fri-Sat 12pm-11.30pm. Rec. dish: Jumbo combo to share £13.95. House wine: £11.25*

○ Chinese/Oriental

Great Wall Chinese Restaurant
105-109 Lothian Road (0131) 229 7747
Fully decked out courtesy of the 'build your own Chinese restaurant in ten easy steps' warehouse, this place is your archetypal example of the genre. It's main selling point is its size so you're looking at at least four hen parties and a group of loud sixteen year olds trying to get away with ordering a round of vodkas and one portion of fried rice. The food isn't bad but it's not the most inspiring place or the best value. Worth a visit for the comedy value of raucous groups upsetting elderly diners. Hilarious.
Mon-Fri 12pm-2pm, 4.30pm-12am
Sat 12pm-12am, Sun 1pm-11.30pm
Cheap eats: Business lunch £5.50 Mon-Fri
Rec. dish: Coconut chicken £8.35
House wine: £10.55

Wok Bar

30 Potterow (0131) 667 8594

Packed with students and hip young things grabbing a bite to eat before they head off to drink pints with gin chasers and grope each other. Enter this screaming blue and orange restaurant and check out the huge array of oriental offerings – everything from Thai to Malaysian and Indonesian to Korean is covered with a flourish (the open kitchen offers some added spectacle). Portions are sizeable and there'll be plenty of change left for that rickshaw home. Modern, fun and good value... give this place a try. Go on.

Mon-Thu 12pm-10.30pm, Fri-Sat 12pm-11pm, Sun 4pm-10.30pm
Cheap eats: Two course lunch for £6.95
Recommended dish: Nasi Goreng £7.25
House wine: £11.95

○ French

Café Grande

182-184 Bruntsfield Place (0131) 228 1188

A relaxed Bruntsfield bistro offering averagely priced grub of the kind slightly better than you might cook at home, and slightly less exciting than you'd usually bother going out for. We're basically talking simple French dishes for people who are too lazy to chop onions themselves. There's nothing to shout about here – not even if we try really hard to find something horrendously negative or positive just for the sake of this review. Umm, one of the waiters has got a shit haircut... See what we mean?

Mon-Wed 9am-11pm, Thu-Sat 9am-12am
Sun 10am-10pm
Recommended dish: Bacon salad £6
House wine: £9.90

Café Marlayne

76 Thistle Street (0131) 226 2230

Handily located off the main city thoroughfares, and as such devoid of confused looking tourists, Café Marlayne has carved itself a niche in Edinburgh's restaurant scene. A little French haven offering well presented and delicious classics – book in advance or you'll never get a table. One of our reviewers tried to make us write that this place constitutes true perfection – we reckon that kind of gushing might be going a bit too far. Add on a brisk rub down from the celebrity of our choice, an ironing service and a free giraffe and we might go with it. As it stands it's just very, very good.

Tue-Sat 12pm-2pm, 6.30pm-10pm. Closed Sun/Mon. Rec. dish: Fillet of beef with mushrooms and roasted garlic £12.90
House wine: £11.50

Café Rouge

Fredrick Street (0131) 225 4515

If you're reading this to get a feel for the place then you must be a foreign tourist. If you're French we advise you stop right now. Not because we're about to slate the cuisine of your fine and glorious country but because this Franglais excuse for a French café would make your grandmother turn in her grave. If

indeed the old dear is actually in one. Café Rouge – seen one, seen 'em all. Not bad for coffee, hot chocolate or a bowl of frites, but if you're expecting authentic culinary expertise you took a wrong turn at Calais.
Mon-Sun 10am-12pm, 5pm-11pm
Recommended dish: 10oz steak £10.95
House wine: £9.95

Jacques
8 Gillespie Place (0131) 229 6080
Avert your eyes from the gaudy décor and breathe in (the seating is rammed in like there was a two for one on tables and chairs at Ikea), we reckon you'll like this authentically French eatery. Forever teeming with pre and post-theatre banter (in festival season it is always packed) Jacques is a little Gallic haven away from the hustle and bustle of Tollcross. On the menu you'll find a range of seafood, meat and game options (not much for veggies – be warned). Nothing fancy, but good solid home cooking.
Mon-Sat 12pm-2.30pm, 5.30pm-11pm
Cheap eats: 5.30pm-7pm, 10pm-11pm.
Rec dish: Cassoulett £20.95 (as part of set three course meal). House wine: £9.25

Maison Bleue
36/38 Victoria Street (0131) 226 1900
Maison Bleue kind of forgets that it's a restaurant half way through your meal. The starters and desserts are fantastic, but give them more than four customers at any one

time and the main courses end up tasting like a four year old was let loose on your order with only a blow torch and a whisk to hand. Plus service can be stupendously slow – we waited 45 minutes for our desserts last time we were in. I mean, 45 minutes? We could build a life-size model of Janet Jackson in that time. It can be a good place to eat (not that we've made it sound like it is) but you really have to pick your moment.
Mon-Sun 12pm-3pm, 5pm-11pm
Cheap eats: Sun-Thu 5pm-7pm 3 courses £9.90. Rec. dish: Duck Confit £9.90
House wine: £9.95

○ Indian

Bangalore
52 Home Street (0131) 229 1348
Drink ten pints of lager, challenge the bloke next to you to an arm wrestle, persist in call-

ing him soft until well after everyone else has started talking about something else, develop an obsession with rugby and chant tunelessly at the top of your voice before entering. You should fit in just about perfectly. While this place has its benefits (they can be arsed to tolerate drunken groups for one) to try and describe the food as anything other than wimpy and lacking authenticity would be a blatant lie. And we don't do lies at itchy.

Sun-Thu 5pm-12am, Fri-Sat 5pm-1am
Cheap eats: 20% discount for students, children eat free on Sunday. Rec. dish: Garlic chicken £5.95. House wine: £9.95

Bombay Bicycle Club
6 Brougham Street (0131) 229 3839

At last, an Indian restaurant where the food tastes of something; at the BBC it's all hot, authentic, unusual and downright delicious. Good for celeb spotting, if there's a star in town and they're up for eating Indian, you'll find 'em here. No need to be on your best behaviour though as this place is as relaxed and atmospheric as they come. You won't be disappointed, we promise.

Mon-Sun 12pm-2pm, 5pm-12am
Rec. dish: Chicken jhilley jhulley £7.95
House wine: £8.95

Guru Balti
9 Dundee Terrace (0131) 221 9779

This is basically your classic Indian restaurant. It's got it all, the dodgy décor, the slightly crazed looking waiters, massive portions and less than salubrious clientele. For your bog standard post-pub curry it's just the ticket. Plus they'll let you take your leftovers home in a doggy bag, so that's breakfast the next morning sorted as well. Classy.

Tue/Wed/Thu/Sun 5pm-11pm, Fri-Sat 5pm - 12am. Cheap eats: Tue and Thu 5pm-12am
Rec. dish: King prawn jayturi £10.95. House wine £9.95

Kalpna
2/3 St Patricks Square (0131) 667 9890

Tree-hugging, vegetarian shoe-wearing, hippy heaven. The rest of you will probably like it too – the food's meat-free, delicious and very authentic. To be fair its popularity

speaks for itself – it's pretty clear no-one ever came here for the décor or to chat up the waiting staff. Still, for a bargain buffet lunch (and a laugh at the hilariously rude menu) you're sorted.

Mon-Sat 12pm-2.30pm, 5.30pm-11pm, Sun 5.30pm-11pm. Cheap eats: Buffet lunch £5
Rec. dish: Dam aloo kassi £7.50
House wine: £9.95

O Italian

Bar Italia
100 Lothian Road (0131) 228 6379
This centrally located Italian joint is consistently busy, noisy and full of energy, and so it should be. The food is fresh, tasty and cheap and if you rock up with twenty mates they won't even bat an eyelid. As such it's perfect for birthday celebrations with plenty of banter and enthusiastic renditions of Happy Birthday the minute you even hint at the concept of a special occasion. It's very much a tuck in, chill out and do whatever you fancy kind of place – if that means you want sparklers in your ice-cream and the waiter with the bushy eyebrows to snog your mate, we reckon they'll probably oblige. Certainly not quiet first-date territory.
Sun-Mon 12pm-3am. Rec. dish: Taglietelle bar Italian £7.50. House wine: £12.50

Bar Roma
39a Queensferry Street (0131) 226 2977
There must be some kind of rule book somewhere that states all cities must have a mini-chain of cheery, inexpensive Italian restaurants. The tourists love 'em and for those days when we lose all sense of personality and imagination, the rest of us love 'em too. Bar Roma is Scotland/Edinburgh's offering – check out the butch waiters, simple menu and comedy group of confused looking Japanese girls at the next table. You could do worse than find yourself here on a night out, but you won't be winning any prizes for originality.
Sun-Thu 12pm-12am, Fri-Sat 12pm-1am
Rec. dish: Spaghetti scoglio £9.95
House wine: £10.95

Caffé Uno
130 High Street (0131) 220 4445
Anything on the Royal Mile needs to really be considered tourist trap first, restaurant second. Caffé Uno makes a brave stab at both offering traditional Italian fare and the tourist friendly salads, baked potatoes and the like. Like everywhere on the Mile it remains busy and bustling (not to mention noisy) whatever the time of year it is but slightly less hectic than some of its neighbours. Not the best place in town by any stretch of the imagination, but by no means the worst.
Sun-Thu 9am-10pm, Fri-Sat 9am-11pm
Rec. dish: Club sandwich £5.95
House wine: £9.70

Est Est Est
135a George Street (0131) 225 2555
One of the better chains (yes, we reckon it's official, 9 out of 10 chain restaurants are Italian) Est Est Est boasts a light and airy space and a nice range of traditional Italian dishes. It's one of those OK but uninspiring places. A safe option for people who drive a Volvo, have pension plans, mortgages and a range of ISAs. There are crayons on offer if you fancy showing off your artistic skills while you wait for your dinner, though chances are you'll be too busy talking your date through the benefits of life insurance to get stuck into anything so frivolous.
Mon-Sun 12pm-11pm. Cheap eats: 2pm-5pm selected main courses £6.95
Rec. dish: Fillet with pepper £15.95
House wine: £10.95

Il Castello
34-36 Castle Terrace (0131) 229 2730

Possibly the friendliest Italian restaurant in Edinburgh, and trust us that takes some doing. Food (pizza, pasta and more classic dishes) and service are fantastic and they showed the footy all the way through the World Cup, which won them a few brownie points with us. The new open kitchen offers a bit of random entertainment and the place still attracts plenty of local custom. That's not to say we recommend you come here to avoid the tourist contingent – they still find their way here somehow.
Mon-Sun 12pm-2.30pm, 5pm-11pm
Recommended dish: Agnolotti £6.95
House wine: £9.80 (for a litre)

Made in Italy
42 Grassmarket (0131) 622 7328

A glorified takeaway in that bizarre Grassmarket area that flips character from charming shopping area to part-time hell-hole depending on the time of day/night. Made in Italy offers bog standard pizza and pasta basics, a bit of naff Italian telly and big streetside windows. Its main pulling factor is its prices – cheap as you like for what you get – and the handy central location.
Mon-Thu 8am-11pm, Fri-Sat 8pm-2am
Sun 8am-11pm. Rec. dish: Pizza £5
House wine: £3.80

Escape the kitchen

Mamma's

30 Grassmarket (0131) 225 6464
1 Howard Street (0131) 558 7177

Renowned for its weird and wonderful pizza toppings this is the ideal place to take odd, awkward or pregnant pals as you can order your pick of 54 diverse toppings for your giant Mamma's secret sauce covered base. So was that one cheese free banana and veggie pizza for your vegan friend and a cactus, olive and chocolate one with extra cheese for the large bellied lady at the back. Right?!

Sun-Thu 12pm-11pm, Fri-Sat 12pm-12am,
Cheap eats: 10% off for students, groups of
10/12 – £6 per head deal
Rec. dish: Panzerotti £7.95
House wine: £8.95

Pizza Express

1 Denhaugh Street (0131) 332 7229
23 North Bridge (0131) 557 6411
32 Queensferry Street (0131) 225 8863

Still protests that its pizzas haven't shrunk and still we insist that they have – we've started a log-book (we're the ones hiding at the back, looking confused with a ruler and a piece of string) and we're going to get it proved once and for all in time for itchy 2004. Size issues aside Pizza Express has plenty to offer – classy buildings, nice design, good service and predictably good food. Ideal for last minute nights out with big groups and stylish shopping lunch breaks. Now where was that protractor?

Mon-Sun 11.30am-11.30pm
Rec. dish: Soho pizza £6.60
House wine: £10.65

Rialto Restaurant

37 Home Street (0131) 229 8386

A family run Italian that still seems to be finding its feet. It's handily located for the Cameo, right by a bus stop and pretty good value. We're not even sure what's lacking but there was something sinister afoot the night we were in. Maybe they just didn't like the look of us, maybe it was a full moon, whatever, we can't explain it so we won't. We reckon you should check this place out for yourself and let us know what your verdict is. We're bored of doing all the hard work... isn't it time you lot gave something back? After all we've done for you? We'll accept cash gifts, diamonds and Matt in our Leeds office quite fancies a PlayStation.

Mon-Sun 10am-12am. Rec. dish: Marinara
£6.95. House wine: £9.50

O Japanese

Yo! Sushi/Yo! Below

66 Rose Street (0131) 220 6040

Brilliant: gather round Edinburgh citizens for at long last we've found somewhere unique, interesting and downright delicious to eat,

drink and hang out. There's that 'waiting for your suitcase at the airport' feeling as the dish you thought had your name on it ends up in the hands of some smug looking bloke at the other end of the room, but it's a small price to pay for such fine Japanese cuisine. For those with a pathological fear of convey- or belts, Yo! Below (the bar bit) has chefs on hand to rustle up anything from sashimi to bento boxes. A handy 'help' button means you can summon staff at a push and a talking robot trolley is also on hand for a novel service option. Whichever side of Yo! you favour, it's a great place for meeting friends and kick-starting a night on the tiles.
Mon-Sun 12pm-11pm. Cheap eats: Mon 6pm-11pm Blue plate special – all dishes £2 Rec. dish: Chicken teriyaki £3 House wine: £11

Bonsai
46 West Richmond St (0131) 668 3847

A conveyor belt-free sushi restaurant – how novel. Bonsai has an impressive selection of expertly prepared sushi and sashimi dishes and remains busy despite its focus on a genre of food that's far too healthy for any self-respecting Scot. Being new and some- what off the beaten track this stylish little venue remains the haunt of Edinburgh's

'those in the know' but given the quality and authenticity of the food this won't be the case for long. Get in there before everyone else does.
Mon-Sat 12pm-late, Sun 5pm-late Rec. dish: Gyoza £3.50. House wine: £9.95

O Mediterranean

Inca
183 Bruntsfield Place (0131) 228 4555
Bypass the snooty Montpeliers next door and step into this trendy Mediterranean restaurant for top-notch food at non-scary prices. Inca is enjoying an enduring populari- ty with Edinburgh's style conscious and no attitude set. Kick back with a classy red and some good sturdy cooking and feel truly smug. Whoever you need to impress, we reck- on you've just struck gold with this place.
Mon-Sun 11am-12am. Cheap eats: 10% student discount on lunch. Rec. dish: Mixed kebab £10.50. House wine £9.25

Phenecia
55 West Nicholson St (0131) 662 4493
Your mate wants Spanish seafood, you fancy a Moroccan tagine and your sister will eat anything as long as it never had eyes... We know that feeling (ok, maybe without the specifics) all too well at itchy. Now normally

we'd favour some kind of fight to the death slanging match before all stomping off home in a huff, swearing never to speak to each other again, but if you fancy dealing with things the civilised way, get in here sharpish. Phenecia offers a massive Mediterranean and North African fusion menu, big portions and plenty of flavour. Booking in advance is pretty essential at weekends and the place is hectic most of the week as well – it's well worth a wait for a table though.

Mon-Sat 12pm-2pm, 6pm-11pm, closed Sunday. Rec. dish: Cous cous £8.90
House wine: £9.55 (per litre) or BYO (£1)

O Mexican

Blue Parrot Cantina
49 St. Stephen Street (0131) 225 2941

Blue Parrot Cantina is like a favourite sibling, it wouldn't matter if they served you up a cardboard box with a topping of sautéed ants, you'd still give them a pat on the back and a big tip at the end of the night. Fortunately though there's no chance of an insect garnished dinner here, the food's spot-on and as near as you'll get to something you'd actually eat in the Yucatan as you'll ever find in frosty Scotland. From the cosy dining room to the beach-themed toilets this places oozes charm, and the enthu-

david bann
vegetarian restaurant & bar
eating and drinking from 11am until 1am open 7 days
56-58 st mary's street, edinburgh
(off the royal mile & the cowgate)
www.davidbann.com
0131 556 5888

No, no, no. Put it away you fool, this ain't no sleazy sauna you know. Rather than ladies of ill-repute, here you'll find some seriously spicy Mexican food, tons of students taking advantage of the prices and the friendliest restaurant owner in town. The location's handy, the vibe is intimate (it's tiny) and buzzy, and the place is packed out every night. Watch out for their no cards policy – it's hard cash all the way in here.
Mon-Sun 6pm-11pm. Rec. dish: Chicken fajitas £10.95. House wine: £7.90

O Scottish

siasm of the staff can't help but rub off on even the moodiest person. Dinner here feels like you just spent a week in Acapulco – chilled, delicious and quite lovely.
Mon-Thu 5pm-11 pm, Fri-Sat 12pm-11pm Sun 5pm-10.30pm. Rec. dish: Fajitas £9 House wine: £8.15

Haw House
44 Candlemaker Row (0131) 220 4420

The Apartment
7-13 Barclay Place (0131) 228 6456
First things first: check out the staff in this place. It's like a local modelling agency just went under and everyone on their books dived into the restaurant next door for a job to tide them over. If you can take your eyes off them for a second and direct them towards the menu you'll find some pleasingly large helpings of Scottish and international dishes all served with a touch of finesse. They have stupid headings on the menu instead of just getting to the point and calling mains 'mains' and starters 'starters'. What is the world coming to? Right, anyway – the

food's good, the décor's minimal posh and it's chilled enough for a casual one. Oh, and did we mention the pretty staff?

Mon-Sat 5.45pm-10.45 pm, Sat-Sun 12pm-3am. Recommended dish: Spicy marinated lamb balls £8.65. House wine £9.90

David Bann
56-58 St Mary's Street (0131) 556 5888

'Vegetarian you say? Like you're ever going to catch me in charge of a plate of alfalfa sprouts and fancy lettuce... I'd get kicked off the pub darts team and everything.' Listen here you, and put the pork scratchings down while we're talking to you; Mr Bann's mouthwatering concoctions will have you converted in no time. Honest. It's great. Offering everything from Thai and veggie burgers to shepherd's pie without the shepherd. Plus there's none of that earth mother type décor either – for once, a veggie joint that doesn't make you feel like some hairy arm-pitted lady is going to rock up any second and demand you pick the cabbages for the commune. Nice one.

Open seven days, 11am-1am
Recommended dish: Malaysian vegetable curry £9. House wine: 10.80

Beluga Canteen Restaurant
30a Chambers Street (0131) 624 4545

Upstairs from the style bar of the same name, the Beluga Canteen offers an equally slick chrome and glass setting in which to sample some fantastic food. From the exotic (Hoi Sin duck with Thai vegetables and spicy mash) to the classic (grilled halibut with spinach and mash in a sweet peppered sauce) there's plenty on offer and portions are anything but supermodel sized. Add to this the fact that you can simply roll down the stairs for drinks afterwards (there's also a handy cash machine) and you've got a spot on night out.

Mon-Thu 12pm-2.30pm, 5.30pm-10pm
Fri-Sun 12pm-2.30pm, 5.30pm-10.30pm
Cheap eats: £9.95 for 2 courses before 8pm
Recommended dish: Duckling leg £15.95
House wine: £11.75

BELUGARESTAURANT

AA ROSETTE STATUS [AWARDED MARCH 2002]
SCOTLAND'S BEST NEW BAR OF THE YEAR 2001-2002 [THEME AWARDS]
SCOTLAND'S CONTEMPORARY BAR OF THE YEAR 2001-2002 [THE DRAM AWARDS]
VISITSCOTLAND AND TASTE OF SCOTLAND ACCREDITED

BOOKBELUGA: 0131 624 4545

BELUGA BAR & RESTAURANT
30a Chambers Street, Edinburgh
www.beluga-edinburgh.com

Blonde

75 St. Leonards Street (0131) 668 2917

Proving that blondes really do have more fun, this place packs in a flash crowd from open to close. You'll find swanky, stylish, polished dishes (amazing seafood, steaks, venison and so on) and a smart interior. It's definitely somewhere to turn up looking a bit better than you usually do with a head full of scintillating conversational ideas to throw to the floor. If you rock up drunk in your football shorts they'll probably still be nice to you but we'd be so ashamed we'd have to stop your pocket money.

Tue-Sun 12pm-2.30pm, 6pm-10pm, Mon 6pm-10pm. Rec. dish: Venison with wine, chilli and chocolate £9.95. House wine: £7.90

Creelers

3 Hunter Square (0131) 220 4447

A top choice for seafood with an ever-changing menu (they have their own smokehouse and another branch on the Isle of Arran) and plenty of traditional and modern takes on fish. The prices are of the 'let's complain about the price of fish' ilk but well worth the credit card bill at the end of the month. Service is friendly rather than the often found 'classy restaurant snootiness'. Really you can't go wrong.

Mon/Thu/Fri 12pm-2pm, 5.30pm-10.30pm, Tue/Wed 5.30pm-10.30pm (lunch Mar-Nov only), Sat-Sun 12.30pm-3pm, 5.30pm-11.30pm. Cheap eats: Mon/Thu/Fri 12pm-2pm, Sat-Sun 12.30pm-3pm

Rec. dish: Hand-dived seared king scallops £17.50. House wine: £11.95

Dial

44-46 George IV Bridge (0131) 225 7179

Apparently there are still people in Edinburgh who actually think this place's interior is the height of modern style. It is your duty to seek them out and inform them that though there's nothing wrong with the place, it was designed in the mid 90s, which can hardly constitute cutting-edge style. Still, you're not here to eat the tables are you? Food wise you'll find fussy, flavoursome and at times downright obscure offerings. Take a group if you can as it's often too quiet to conjure up a properly buzzing atmosphere.

Mon-Sun 12pm-3pm, 6pm-11pm

Cheap eats: Pre-theatre deal £10.95, party deal (2 courses + half bottle of wine) £16.50

Rec. dish: Filleted Aberdeen Angus beef £18.95. House wine from £10.95

 the elephant house 21 George VI Bridge 0131 220 5355

Fishers in the City
58 Thistle Street (0131) 225 5109

An offshoot from the Leith Fishers, Fishers in the City gives us metropolitan types a chance to sample their inventive fish dishes. The menu changes daily offering the freshest, seasonal sea creatures and there's always a couple of non-fish options for those of you that are stupid enough to turn up somewhere like this when you don't like fish. It's not even stupidly expensive: give it a go.
Mon-Sat 12pm-10.30pm, Sun 12.30pm-10.30pm. Rec. dish: Fishcake soup £3.75. House wine: £9.95

Hadrian's
Balmoral Htl, 1 Princes St (0131) 557 5000

Hadrian's is an outpatient from the local psychiatric hospital – it thinks it's Eton educated and seventh in line to the throne. The vibe is formal, aloof and verging on snooty, but the food is low key and at surprisingly state school prices. Come here for fuss-free bistro fare and old school service.
Mon-Sat 7am-10.30am, 12pm-2.30pm, 6pm-10.30pm, Sun 7.30am-11am, 12.30pm-3pm, 6pm-10.30pm. Cheap eats: Lunch £7.99 (2 courses), Dinner £10.99 (3 courses). Rec. dish: Salmon £8.50. House wine: £14

Heights
Apex International Hotel
31-35 Grassmarket (0131) 473 7156

Heights have done you proud on the location front (it's at the top of the Apex Hotel) and though you'll be more likely to bump into Larry from Los Angeles than Layla from Leith it's well worth a visit. Like many of Edinburgh's better restaurants Heights errs on the formal side – turn up in your Dad's old jumper with last night's curry stains and we guarantee you'll feel like a leper. This is somewhere to wine, dine, romance and draw out the civilised conversationalist that lies within all of us. Oh, and the food (classy meat and fish dishes mainly) is excellent.
Mon-Sat 7pm-10pm, lunches appointment only. Cheap eats: Monthly offers. Rec. dish: Sea Bass £14.95. House wine: £12.50

(i) Recommended

Posh Nosh
- Hadrian's
- Oloroso
- Point Restaurant
- The Tower
- Witchery

Howies

10-14 Victoria Street (0131) 225 1721
208 Bruntsfield Place (0131) 221 1777
4–6 Glanville Place (0131) 225 5553
29 Waterloo Place (0131) 556 5766

It's all change at Howies. The four Edinburgh branches have had a bit of a reshuffle with Howies Victoria and Howies Waterloo Place opening recently. Meanwhile the St Leonard's Street branch has been leased to another restaurant and the Dalry Road branch has become The Flaming Red Dining Room (see separate entry). All four restaurants share the same respect for clean unfussy design and high quality inventive grub (or "fine food without the faff" as their motto goes) at reasonable prices. It's all very fresh (excellent seafood and game) and where possible, locally sourced. Each venue manages to retain its own vibe and the menus vary slightly under each chef – regardless though you'll find wicked set menu deals, a 45-minute lunch option and a bargainous wine list (there's also BYO). A true (and some would say passé) Edinburgh institution.

Mon-Sun 12pm-2.30pm, 6pm-10pm (Victoria, Bruntsfield and Glanville)
Mon-Sun 10am-12pm, 12pm-2.30pm, 6pm-10.30pm (Waterloo Place). Cheap eats: Sun-Thu £11.95 3 courses before 7.30pm
Rec. dish: Duck breast with liquor sauce.
House wine from £7.90

Indigo Yard

7 Charlotte Lane (0131) 220 5603

Crazily popular and just about worth the fight for a table if you like Oriental-tinged food, cocktails and the smell of crisp banknotes as they exit your wallet. Whether you come for breakfast, lunch or dinner the place is sure to be filled with city boy types guffawing loudly about share prices and the joy of being absolutely bloody loaded. If you don't have it in you to rise above it then you might want to give this one a miss. If you can manage to zone out or you actually are a guffawing business type who likes nothing more than comparing pay packets over a spot of lunch then this posers' paradise will suit you down to the ground.

Mon-Sun 8.30am-10pm (bar 'til 1am or 3am during Christmas/Festival). Cheap eats: Weekday lunch – 2 courses including coffee £8.95. Rec. dish: Spiced red coconut and coriander chicken £6.25.
House wine from £11.50

Montpeliers

159-161 Bruntsfield Plce (0131) 229 3115
Run by the same people as Indigo Yard and equally stuffed to the brim with the kind of folk who are more interested in what the person next to them is wearing than having

a good time. This is one of those places where if you're in, you're in, and if you're not everyone stares at you like you just marched in like you own the place with a recently slaughtered baby seal slung over your shoulder. Snobby, snooty and downright boring which is a shame as the food is actually pretty decent, but we'd rather eat spam straight from the tin for the rest of our lives than endure this place ever again.
Mon-Sun 9am-10pm (bar 12.30pm-1am) Rec. dish: Chicken breast with lemon and ginger, mash potato and green beans (£6.45 day menu, £8.95 eve menu) House wine: £10.95

Opal Lounge
51 George Street (0131) 226 2275

In contrast to your Indigo Yards and your Montpeliers this place manages to be aspirational without being obnoxious. Buzzy, busy and something a bit different, it's ideal for a night out with your cooler mates – the food is wicked and the vibe is always upbeat. Even better the bar is fantastic with top notch DJs and wicked swanky cocktails. Plus (don't roll your eyes, we know you love this kind of shit)

apparently the pin-up prince (Wills) himself has eaten here – if Opal Lounge is good enough for our future King, surely, but surely it's good enough for us.
Mon-Sun 12pm-3am. Rec. dish: Pork and egg noodles £6.95. House wine: £11.95

Parrots
3 Viewforth (0131) 229 3252
This bizarre parrot themed bistro serves up good cocktails, gorgeous calorie laden desserts and solid, pub grub kinda food to a bizarre mix of characters. As a result you'll find this place (rather refreshingly we reckon) devoid of any of your classic Edinburgh 'types'. Plus there's plenty of opportunity for lame dad-style jokes about whether you are or are not looking at someone else's bird. Really quite decent in a surreal kind of way.
Tue-Thu 6pm-late, Fri-Sat 5.30pm-late Cheap eats: Members 10% discount (life membership £25). Rec. dish: Beef and three mustards £7.45. House wine: £9

Point Restaurant
34 Bread Street (0131) 221 5555
Super stylish inside and out. Point is one of those special occasions kind of places that pulls people back for more with a chilled out

ease. The food is a good value mix of modern classics and the odd exotic dish to inspire you away from the steak. The only negative is that like most hotel restaurants Point does feel a bit like, well, a hotel restaurant. Don't let that put you off though – it's handy for the rest of Edinburgh nightlife and well worth a look.

Mon-Sat 1pm-3pm, 6pm-10pm (Sun 'til 11pm). Cheap eats: 3 courses £14.90 Rec. dish: Fish special £14.90 (as part of 3 courses). House wine from £10.95

Smoke Stack
53-55 Broughton Street (0131) 556 6032

Work nights out and birthday bashes sorted. Smoke Stack serves up quality American (with a Scottish twist) style grill dishes (mainly meat – steaks and the like), slurringly potent cocktails and a hefty dose of atmosphere to a loud, lively crowd most nights. It's definitely best enjoyed with a group, but if you can't resist the lure of the food (it really is that good) and you're on a date, ask to be seated in the slightly more secluded lower level. Smoke Stack is one of those places that doesn't pretend to be anything it's not (no poncey style statements and posturing waiting staff) and as a result excels at what it does best. Top notch.

Mon-Fri 12pm-2.30pm, 6pm-10.30pm Sat 12pm-10.30pm, Sun 6pm-10.30pm Cheap eats: Lunch menu offers Mon-Fri 12pm-2pm. Rec. dish: Sirloin steak £12.95. House wine: £9.95

The Tower
Museum of Scotland, Chambers Street (0131) 225 3003

Ultra stylish and nestling at the top of the Museum of Scotland this place has amazing views, modern design and a unique vibe. The intimate feel and acceptable pricing suits ladies that lunch, business types and those looking for romance in equal measures. Take a date here and we guarantee they'll put out afterwards – the food is fantastic (subtle, inventive, insert your own superlative here), the feel is calm, relaxing and truly special. Students and skint people should steer rich uncles or proud parents in this direction next time they're in town and offering to foot the bill for dinner. Properly impressive.

Mon-Sun 12pm-11pm. Rec. dish: Salmon parcel £15.95. House wine: £13.75

The Witchery
352 Castlehill, Royal Mle (0131) 225 5613

For some The Witchery is the epitome of style, for others it's just plain terrifying – all that wine list and trying to understand what samphire is stuff can really take it out of a person. Still, it would be churlish to try and find fault with what is quite honestly the most spectacular restaurant in town, and like nowhere else. The food is ridiculously impressive, the feel is romantic, intimate and truly special and the décor is a hotch-potch, but style conscious mix, of antiques, candles and random stencilling. This is somewhere for special occasions, so get all ideas of rocking up out of your box at ten to eleven looking for a curry out of your head.

Sun-Sat 12pm-4pm, 5.30pm-11.30pm
Cheap eats: 2 course £9.95 light lunch/theatre supper (available daily 12pm-4pm, 5.30pm-6.30pm & 10.30pm-11.30pm)
Rec. dish: Sea breem with rosemary cream £17.50. House wine from £13.75

○ Spanish

La Tasca
9 South Charlotte Street (0131) 220 0011
Greenside Place Omni Ctr (0131) 558 8894

OK, so it may not beat relaxing with a rioja or chewing on chorizo in the old streets of Barcelona or Madrid, but for a taste of Spain in Auld Reekie then this is as close as you're going to get to the real deal. Both venues can accommodate large parties so if you're looking to hold a birthday or work's bash then this is the place to head. If you contact the restaurant in advance you can even arrange for a menu to suit your taste(s). There are numerous Spanish tapas dishes and a fine selection of wines to work your way through, and since prices start from a couple of pounds a dish you can afford to experiment a little.

Mon-Sun 12pm-11pm (Charlotte St)
Mon-Sun 12pm-12am (Greenside Place)
Rec. dish: Meat paella £8.95 per person, veg paella £7.95. House wine: £9.45

Ayutthaya
14b Nicholson Street (0131) 556 9351

We'd love to buck the trend of a million and one rave reviews. In fact we're sure Ayutthaya has an entire encyclopaedic library of positive press and might even welcome the excitement of a bad review. Still, we'll be vilified by the obsessed Ayutthaya mafia if we so much as criticise the shape of their knives,

so we'll stick with towing the party line for now. Not a tough job as this place is out of this world – gorgeous food, a serene vibe and polite yet friendly service. The banquet menus are top-notch and the Tom Kar Gai soup has to go down in history as the finest we've ever tasted. In fact if Ayutthaya was a cult we'd be first in the line for membership. Spot on and does takeaway too.

Mon-Sun 12pm-3pm, 5.30pm-11pm Cheap eats: Banquet for 2 (3 courses and coffee) £36. Rec. dish: Gaung keow wan £7.70. House wine: £8.95

Sukothai
23 Brougham Place (0131) 229 1537
The run down sibling of Ayutthaya offers the same fantastic Thai cuisine and handy central location but with less of the glamour. It's kind of the Billie Piper to Ayutthaya's Britney Spears but well worth a visit all the same. Like its more successful sister the food is properly spot-on and totally addictive.

Mon-Sun 12pm-2.30pm, 5.30pm-10.30pm Meal for two: £30-35 (Nam prig ong)

Thai Orchid
14 Grindlay Street (0131) 228 4438
Under Scottish-Thai management Thai Orchid is the most vibrantly decorated Thai restaurant in Edinburgh. Five minutes in this place and the Scottish rain will be nothing but a distant memory. Food is elegant and

THAI ORCHID

Authentic Thai Cuisine in Elegant Surroundings

44 Grindlay Street Edinburgh
0131 228 4438

delicious and the feel is upbeat. Good for first dates and relaxed bargain lunches.

Mon-Fri 12pm-2.30pm, 5.30pm-12am, Sat 5.30pm-12pm. Cheap eats: Banquet for 2 (3 courses) £21.95 per person. Rec. dish: Green chicken curry £7.95. House wine: £9.95

bars

www.itchyedinburgh.co.uk

Bam Bou
66-67 South Bridge (0131) 556 0200

Bam Bou is one of those bars that kind of does your head in. The music is decent enough – plenty of variety and DJs that know their tunes – the crowd is friendly and the location is handily central. Yet somehow it misses the point – by miles. You won't be able to put your finger on it; you'll just know there's something not quite right here. Maybe we're wrong, maybe our mates spike our drinks with sinister hallucinogenics whenever we go to the toilet, but we're just not feeling the vibe.

Mon-Sun 11am-1am. Happy Hour: Various drinks offers from 75p. Food: 12pm-4pm. Rec. dish: Lasagne £4.25, 2 course special deal £4.95, House Wine: £11.45

Bar: Alba
11-13 Grassmarket (0131) 229 2665

Where do all the old men drink now they've been turfed out of their haunts in favour of the style bar rent-a-crowd? This pre-club bar pulls in a mix of wannabe mover and shaker types to drink fancy beverages and engage each other in inane banter about how cool their lives are with alarming regularity. Uncle Burt would turn in his grave.

Mon-Sat 11am-1am, Sun 12pm-1am. Food: Mon-Sun 12pm-9pm. Rec. dish: Tortilla wraps £4.95, House Wine: £9.50

Bar Kohl
54 George IV Bridge (0131) 225 6936

Recently expanded, a night out in Bar Kohl is now a little less like getting drunk in a corridor. Revelling in the new-found expanse you'll find a happy blend of posh students and trendy nine-to-fivers. Join them to knock

Baroque
39 Broughton Street (0131) 557 0627

Right, it's on Broughton Street, so they were never going to have a problem pulling a crowd, but things are looking more than a little rough around the edges here. Baroque would have you believe it's the love-child spawn of Gaudi himself, but the overall effect is just plain gaudy. Sometimes lived-in works but the previous tenants in this joint appear to be of the skanky, unclean type and frankly, it just doesn't. Not for us anyway... and we're the experts after all. Apparently anyway.

Mon-Sun 10am-1am. Happy Hour: Fri 4pm-7pm 2-4-1 on all drinks except cocktails and champagnes. Food: 10am-10pm. Rec. dish: Chicken sweetcorn chowder and special sauce £7.95, House Wine: £10.50

back vodkas from the stupidly long list and get down to a funky hip hop sound track. Just a hunch but we think you'll like it here.
Mon-Sat 11.30am-1am. Food: 11.30am-3pm. Rec. dish: Vodka burger £6.25, House Wine: £10.80

bar : alba

Mon-Sat 11am-1am
Sun 12pm-1am
11-13 Grassmarket (0131) 229 2665

BELUGABAR

AA ROSETTE STATUS [AWARDED MARCH 2002]
SCOTLAND'S BEST NEW BAR OF THE YEAR 2001-2002 [THEME AWARDS]
SCOTLAND'S CONTEMPORARY BAR OF THE YEAR 2001-2002 [THE DRAM AWARDS]
VISITSCOTLAND AND TASTE OF SCOTLAND ACCREDITED

BARFOOD SERVED 9AM-9PM

BELUGA BAR & RESTAURANT
30a Chambers Street, Edinburgh
T: 0131 624 4545 www.beluga-edinburgh.com

Bar 38
126-128 George Street (0131) 220 6180
When Bar 38 opened, much was made of the unisex Ally McBeal style toilets. We reckon it won't be too long before 38 goes the same way as the stick thin whingeing one... the cracks are starting to show – so beware of the fall out. We're talking mismatch décor, try-hard desperadoes in every corner and a distinct feeling of overwhelming mediocrity that no amount of hard drinking can shake off, however hard you try.
Mon-Sat 11am-1am, Sun 11am-12am
Happy Hour: 5pm-7pm every day, deals on cocktails and pitchers. Food: all day
Rec. dish: Chilli, chicken and orange £6.25, House Wine: £11.95

The Basement
10a-12a Broughton St (0131) 557 0097
See what they've done with the name? Pure genius. Now, imaginative monikers aside, this place is actually pretty decent. Ignore the garish orange and blue décor and slide your way to the bar for a few shots of premium tequila. Now look again – suddenly you come round to their way of thinking. If not repeat step one until you do. Drinking advice aside there's plenty to entertain you here. Try the Mexican and Thai food, tap your feet to the funky tunes or just take the piss out of the bar staff's hideous Hawaiian shirts.
Mon-Sun 12pm-1am. Food: 12pm-10.30pm
Rec. dish: Different themes each day, average £4.95 main course. Business lunch 2 meals for 1 £6.95. House Wine: £9.50

Beluga
30a Chambers street (0131) 624 4545
A Sex in the City style bar set in a one time dental hospital. No longer pulling teeth but definitely pulling the punters, this place is young, cool and still hugely popular with th

All dressed up and somewhere to go

Edinburgh stylish crew. We're talking classy cocktails, posh food and swanky punters – perfect for satisfying that need for unadulterated glamour and class that languishes deep within all of us. Admire the extravagant water feature, check out the sickeningly good looking bar staff and join us in the bar queue – we'll be the ones looking a bit confused and waiting to get chucked out for being too common.

Mon-Sun 9am-1am. Food: Bar 9am-10pm, Rest 12pm-2.30pm & 5.30pm-9.45pm ('til 10.30pm Fri-Sat). Rec. dish: Spinach, wild mushroom, Lanark blue & watercress mash £12.75, House Wine: £11.75

Pre Jazz Menu
served at biblos

Food served until midnight
Sunday to Thursday
and till 9pm Friday & Saturday
£1 off entry to beat jazz basement with meal receipt
open 9am-1am 7 days a week
1 chambers street, edinburgh
t: 0131 226 7177 www.festival-inns.co.uk/biblos

but you'll find this place exudes an unexpected level of sophistication. Not, we might add, in a let's all compare wallets for fun kind of way, but in a laid back, grown up, let's drink, dance and talk about the old days 'til they kick us out sort of way. Great stuff.
*Mon-Sat 5pm-3am (Fri 4pm-3am).
Food: Buffets for parties on request,
House Wine: £12*

Berlin Bierhaus

3 Queensferry St Lane (0131) 467 7215

If you've been lucky enough to acquire some friends over the years who are interesting enough to actually sit down and listen to once in a while you might want to bring them here. The name may conjure up images of beer-bellied Germans knocking back flagons of Warsteiner with their Sauerkraut,

Biblos

1 Chambers Street (0131) 226 7177

Perfect for those who want to see and be seen (not an option for two-timing skivers) this big-windowed corner bar is one of Edinburgh's latest offerings. Things seem to be shaping up well – come here for beats,

ones. Well worth checking out – once you do you'll be a part of the furniture before you know it.

Mon-Fri 11am-11pm, Sat-Sun 10am-11pm Food: 11am-10pm. Rec. dish: Chicken enchilada £5.95, House Wine: £9.95

The Brass Monkey
14 Drummond Street (0131) 556 1961

Once a proper old Scottish boozer, now one of those fancy studenty pub/bars that everyone likes to complain about. As much as we'd like to join the protest and start a campaign to banish all those irreverent, hard-drinking student types from the city forever, there's no denying that this is a pretty fine place. Top marks for the cinema room, which shows free films all day, spot-on music policy, pool room, fireplace and relaxed vibe. With all this on offer you won't even notice all the essay-deadline whingeing. Honest.

Mon-Sat 11am-1am, Sun 12pm-12am Food: Bar snacks, House Wine: £8.95

Candy Bar
113-115 George Street (0131) 225 9179

Take one Glasgow success story, place on ultra-trendy George Street, add a locust-like swarm of Edinburgh's pretty people and you

eats and a cool but decidedly non-cliquey feel. The window seats are top of everyone's list of priorities so expect sneering looks and general disdain should you be lucky enough to bag them. If you do manage to grab 'em then you'll be there all night – promise.

Mon-Sun 8am-1am. Food: Sun-Thu 8am-12am, Fri-Sat 8am-9pm. Rec. dish: Steak sandwich £7.55, House Wine: £10.50

Blue Moon Café
36 Broughton Street (0131) 556 2788

In a city rapidly disappearing under a mountain of style bars it comes as a great relief to still see places like this going strong. Blue Moon is not only an Edinburgh institution, it's also the cosiest venue around. The staff are refreshingly friendly and forever engaging in banter with customers, whether you're a new face or one of the many regular

have the recipe for yet another success story. As we go to press Candy Bar has not long opened her Edinburgh doors, and so far both the bar and her clientele are looking good.
Mon-Sun 11am-1am. Rec. dish: Candy special (grilled chicken, smoked bacon, tomato) £5.95, House Wine: £11.95

Centraal

38 West Nicolson St (0131) 667 7355
Recently opened in the heart of student pub land, Centraal claims, in an earth-shatteringly original manner, to do alcohol, tobacco and food. You'll find it lives up to these revolutionary claims and is a bit of a hit with your classier (that's clarssier to you) student type.

Décor wise they'll be no great accolades – it's the done before sofas, wood and candles look all the way, but it somehow works. At weekends this place is a roadblock and you'll find yourself stuck in the same spot for most of the night. Rock up midweek if you're too soft to crowd surf back from the bar with your pints.
Mon-Sat 11am-1am, Sun 12.30pm-12am Food: Mon-Sat 11am-11pm, Sun 12.30pm-11pm, Rec. dish: Half kg of mussels £4.70, House Wine: £10.95

City Café

19 Blair Street (0131) 220 0125
This is an American-style diner that actually pre-dates the nationwide epidemic of American-style diners – whooping high-fives all round hey? You'll find it pretty chilled, offering wicked all day breakfasts, burgers and nachos, as well as pool and DJs of comically disputable talent. With drinks around the '£3 are you having a larf?' mark, it is advisable to go for beer over spirits as the latter tend to focus on presentation rather than quantity which, lets face it, is a clash of priorities. Alternatively, rock up for happy hour from 5-8pm.
Mon-Sun 11am-1pm. Happy Hour: 5pm-8pm everyday. Rec. dish: Lamb and rosemary burger with caramelised apples £5.65, House Wine: £9.45 (£6.50 in Happy Hour)

Dome Bar

14 George Street (0131) 624 8624
Swank centralis – this is your classic bank conversion but here you get more than a Wetherspoons two-for-one meal to whet

your appetite. Enter and admire a world of fancy décor, flash food and surprisingly reasonable drinks prices. Leave swiftly, downing your drink in record time, when you realise the place is full of the biggest collection of wannabes, has-beens and never-will-bes you've ever come across. If burrowing up the arse of the person next to you whilst quaffing the lastest drink du jour is your idea of a night on the tiles, you'll love it here.
Mon-Sat 10am 'til late, Sun 12.30pm 'til late
Food: 12pm 'til late, House Wine: £14.50

Edwards
4 South Charlotte Street (0131) 226 5526
Stag and hen night central – as the townie masses bev themselves up in what must be one of the dullest and most uninspiring chain bars around, blue collar lads and lasses blow their monthly wages in one go for the sake of a quick grope, before throwing it all back up again. Redeeming points: umm, it has doors and you can leave by them.
Mon-Sun 12pm-1am. Happy Hour: Sun-Thu 5pm-1am, Fri 5pm-8pm £1.50 selected drinks. Food: Mon-Thu 12.30pm-7pm, Fri-Sun 12.30pm-8pm. Recommend dish: Club sandwich £4.95, House Wine: £10

EH1
197 High Street (0131) 220 5277
Slap bang in the centre of town, EH1 has always been a bit of a cool kid hangout. As time's gone on though, it's faded from the in-crowd radar, leaving behind only die-hard fans and dignified, laid back types that can't handle the ruck at the bar for the new bar of the moment. The club crowd fill the place to bursting at weekends, but weekdays and early evenings are pure quiet pint territory. Something for just about everyone – if you're in the area make sure you drop in.
Mon-Sun 9am-1am. Happy Hour: 5pm-8pm everyday, discounted cocktails and pitchers
Food: Breakfast 9am-12pm, Main menu 12pm-7pm. Rec. dish: Warm chicken, pepper and artichoke salad £4.95
House Wine: £10.95

Favorit
30-32 Leven Street (0131) 221 1800
19 Teviot Place (0131) 220 6880
Another American diner type affair – pricey and predictable, but what does that matter at 2.30am when you'd happily sell all your elderly relatives just to inhale the fumes of a Long Island Iced Tea? Food wise this place

does the usual big American portions and everything from salads to waffles. The Ben & Jerry's milkshakes are worth looking up from your cocktail for and this place is deservedly busy.

Leven St: Mon-Sun 8am-1am (food 'til 1am)
Teviot Pl: Mon-Sun 8.30am-3am (food 'til 2.30am). Rec. dish: Spicy chicken and caesar wrap £3.85, House Wine: £10.70

Frankenstein
26 George IV Bridge (0131) 622 1818
For tonight at least, God is a DJ. In this church conversion you'll find the DJ quite literally preaching from the pulpit. And what does he preach, pray tell? Well, a slightly incongruous brand of vintage 80s pop to a drunken rabble of alcopop downing students, hens and stags, of course. You'll find this place rammed to the holy rafters with people who are far too drunk to even know where they are, let alone care that 'The Sun Always Shines On TV' has just been played for the fourth time. Dark, dingy and dreadfully obvious but there's definitely a time and place for Frankenstein's. If you work it out can you let us know?

Mon-Sun 10am-1am. Happy Hour: Wed 8pm-1am, Fri 5pm-7pm 2-4-1 cocktail pitchers/ beer pitchers. Food: Mon-Sun 10am-1am, Rec. dish: Fajitas £6.95, House Wine: £7.95

Grand Cru
79 Hanover Street (0131) 226 6427
Oooh la-di-da, look at you with your fancy new outfits and perfectly manicured nails. Look how well Daddy's business is doing and how cool and beautiful you are. As you reach into your bag for a deck of Marlboro Lights, flick your highlights over a tanned shoulder and survey the room for talent, don't you just marvel at how wonderful it is that everyone else in here is just as glamorous as you? To think they might have acci-

dentally let some common people in here by mistake. Readers – we'd like to say 'Go forth ugly, poor people, don't be put off by these tales of ostentation' but that would be like sending you to the lions. So we won't.

Sun-Wed 10am-1am, Thu-Sat 10am-2am.
Happy Hour: Mon-Sun 4.30pm-9pm
Food: Mon-Sun 10am-11pm. Rec. dish: Chilli £4.50, House Wine: £9

bar : alba   11-13 Grassmarket (0131) 229 2665

Hamiltons Bar Kitchen
16-18 Hamilton Place (0131) 226 4199
Situated in the heart of fashionable Stockbridge – Edinburgh's answer to Notting Hill – the clientele ranges from trendy young things to business types. Suede cubettes, trendy sofas, stainless steel fittings and retro abstract canvasses are the order of the day. You can sip cocktails, wine and pints in the surprisingly airy lounge or head for the mezzanine level, which provides a more enclosed space if you're after a touch more privacy. Stylish without being pretentious, Hamilton's is one fine venue.
Mon-Sun 11am-1am. Food: Mon-Thu 11am-10pm, Fri-Sat 11am-8pm, Sun 11am-7pm. Rec. dish: Beer battered haddock with thick cut chips £6, House Wine: £10.75

Henry J Beans
Rutland Street (0131) 222 8844
'I'll have a glass of white wine and a hefty dose of sycophantic Americana on the side please.' Check out the décor: licence plates bolted to the walls and photos of some D-list soap star that apparently drank here once. Add to that bar staff who have clearly been trained the Atlantic way – all OTT smiles and constant questions – and you've got a recipe for bad anger management. What miserable Scot can really handle such a level of cheer and/or bear to part with any kind of tip for the privilege of someone's feigned interest. It just don't add up and it just ain't happening. The cocktails are alright though, if you're still listening.
Mon-Sat 12pm-1am, Sun 12.30pm-1am Rec dish: Chicken sandwich £7.25, House Wine: £8.85

Human Be-In
West Crosscauseway (0131) 662 8860
This place doubles up as a second union so you'll find it packed with academic types day in, day out. None of your proper old school students here though, it's more of a ciao-baby-mobile-phoney-daddy's-got-a-Porsche kind of crowd. Don't let this put you off though; they're all far too busy trying to live like common people to even hint at snobbery. Rock up for posh study groups, flash lunch breaks and mingle with the future of our great nation as they cancel afternoon science labs for bottles of foreign lager and celebrity gossip.
Mon-Fri 11am-1am, Sat-Sun 12pm-1am Food: Mon-Fri 11am-9pm, Sat-Sun 12pm-9pm. Rec. dish: Wild game stew £8.95, House Wine: £8.95

Iguana
41 Lothian Street (0131) 220 4288

A summertime magnet for Edinburgh's twenty-something contingent who like to hook themselves up to intravenous G&T drips and bask in the sun outside. Despite sitting on Edinburgh Uni's doorstep, Iguana is not overrun with students. Instead you'll find the local trendy types following a strict regime of fashionable cocktails, fusion bar snacks and DJ beats. Don't bother with the food if you're properly hungry – portions are on the wrong side of small – but do bear this place in mind when late night starvation sets in... they keep serving up 'til 3am.

Sun-Thu 9am-1am, Fri-Sat 9am-3am
Happy Hour: Fri 6pm-9pm. Food served:
Mon-Sun 9am-10pm. Rec. dish: Chicken faji-
tas £6.50, House Wine: £10.95

Indigo Yard
7 Charlotte Lane (0131) 220 5603

If only this were my back yard: cocktails, good grub and delightful staff servicing my every need... well, maybe not every need. Going strong for several years now, Indigo Yard is perennially popular with the out-of-the-office-into-the-bar crowds. And, as this

yard is well and truly protected from the elements, not even the Edinburgh rain need mess up your night. You'll have to do that all by yourself.

Mon-Sun 8.30am-1am. Happy Hour: Fri-Sat 5pm-8pm 2-4-1 on selected spirits and jugs Food: Mon-Sun 8.30am-10pm. Rec. dish: Wild mushroom risotto £5.95 day /£8.75 evening, House Wine: £11.15

La Tasca
9 South Charlotte Street (0131) 220 0011
Greenside Place (0131) 558 8894
How lucky are the Spanish? They have great food, tremendous wine, amazing weather, those sexy Mediterranean features, party all night and go to bed in the afternoon. Well, we might not have the weather, good looks or siestas, but we do now have the food and a place in which to at least pretend that we're in Marbella in the middle of summer. La Tasca serve up a host of tasty Tapas dishes, and they also allow you to relax in the bar with some sumptuous cocktails, a bottle of rioja or a few cold cervezas.

South Charlotte St: Mon-Sun 12pm-11pm Greenside Place: Mon-Sun 12pm-12am Rec. dish: Meat paella £8.95 per person, Veg paella £7.95, House Wine: £9.45

Living Room
235 Cowgate (0131) 225 4628
If it ain't broke why fix it? And if the hotch-potch mix of students and (well the last time we were in anyway) the odd random well-to-do middle aged man are happy to keep coming back year upon year, what would really be the point of a revamp? Living Room dishes out the same hip-hoppy, faux-ironic, happy hours and hair-gel formula it always did and the kids, quite frankly, can't get enough of it. The kids are alright by us.

Mon-Sun 5pm-11pm. Happy Hour: Sun-Thu 5pm-11pm, Fri-Sat 5pm-11pm £1 pt Heineken, £1.50 Stella Artois and Kronenberg, £1 vodka shots and selected alcopops, House Wine: £7.20

Medina
45-47 Lothian Street (ex-directory)
With its spot-on music policy and upbeat vibe, Medina really delivers. It's paid back for its offerings with a constant stream of hip, young things and an ever increasing popularity quotient. Don't mess. If you decide to buck the trend and claim you don't like this place you'll be banished from Edinburgh forever and forced to spend the rest of your days in a small village in the Highlands, making kilts out of goat hair for fun. Don't say we didn't warn you.

Mezz
49-51 London Street (0131) 556 9808
Mezz is one of the new bars in town and rather than nicking its bike and ignoring it in the playground, it appears the good folk of

Broughton have decided to let it get in with the cool crowd. Laid back décor, an arty twist, top notch cocktails and food served in portions that don't evoke instant starvation anxiety. This is the kind of place that just doesn't try too hard and it sure as hell pays off. With such a promising start we can only hope things continue this way.

Mon-Sun 11am-1am. Food: 12pm-7.30pm
Rec. dish: Ginger and garlic breaded prawns
£5.95, House Wine: £10.50

Monboddo
34 Bread Street (0131) 221 5555

Realising that it's not just the paper-pushing, suited-up non-entities of this world who enjoy fine cocktails in swanky surroundings, Monboddo shakes up the spirits at sensible prices. Resembling a New York art gallery with its funky décor, the central bar screams style and a daily happy hour makes a night on the Mojitos even easier to swallow. Aspiring yuppies, and anyone in search of a classy night out, need look no further. Dress to kill, mind your manners, replace your minging-looking partner with someone altogether more glamourous and you'll fit in just fine. Alright?

Mon-Sat 10am-1am, Sun 12pm-1am. Happy
Hour: 5pm-8pm. Food: Mon-Sun 12pm-5pm
Rec. dish: Salmon £4, House Wine: £10.50

The Moo-Bar (Aka The Meadows Bar)
42-44 Buccleuch Street (0131) 667 6907

No longer the seedy, grungy hangout it used to be with a serious make-over under its wings, Moo Bar can't quite live up to the alternative hype. Posh students with travelling tales and Asian symbol tattoos just can't do rock'n'roll. Still, you'll find this somewhere where the music is a little louder and the clientele a little dirtier than everywhere else round here. And this breath of not-so-fresh air is pulling 'em in with drunken regulars spilling in and out every night of the week.

Mon-Sat 11am-1am, Sun 12.30pm-1am Happy Hour: discounts for students all day. Food: Mon-Sun 12pm-4pm. Rec. dish: All under £4, House Wine: £7.95

Native State
32 Potterrow (0131) 662 9788

Yawn. This big, black, shiny style bar serves up pricey drinks, pricey food and loads of shooters for your drinking pleasure. The fireplace offers solace from the great outdoors on wintery evenings – we suggest hanging out here with a nice glass of stout, a pair of slippers and the paper. You won't fit in at all but the look on the faces of the straight-laced clientele will be reward enough for the humiliation. The daily two-for-one breakfast deal between 9am and 11am is well worth a look in for. Check out also the £1 a go shooters on Saturdays.

Mon-Sun 9am-1am. Happy Hour: Fri 4pm-7pm 2-4-1 selected drinks, 7pm-1am shooters £1, Sat 6pm-1am shooters £1, Sun 5pm-1am 2-4-1 cocktails. Food: 9am-12pm Breakfast , full menu 12pm-10pm (Fri-Sat 12pm-9pm). Rec. dish: Homemade burgers from £5.75, House Wine: £9.95

Negociants
45-47 Lothian St (0131) 225 6313

Considering it's virtually located within an Edinburgh Uni lecture theatre, it's not surprising that Negociants is student centralis. With a wide selection of global beers at not so cheap prices (it's hard to know if you're paying for import tax or the entire shipping cost), the students in here tend to hail from leafy estates in the Home Counties rather than high rises in Huddersfield. Still, the atmosphere and clientele are laid back, the snacks tasty and by the time you're turfed out at 3am you won't be able to remember where you live now, let alone where you were born.

Mon-Sun 9am-3am. Happy Hour: Tue/Thu 10pm-3am Admission: Tue/Thu £3, Sat-Sun £2. Food: Mon-Sat 9am-3am, Sun 10am-3am. Rec. dish: Carbonara £5.25 House Wine: white £9.95, red £10.95

Opal Lounge
51 George Street (0131) 226 2275

An initial head round the door doesn't do the Opal Lounge justice. Its 80s Manhattan wine bar feel, coupled with Bostonian booths make the place Easton-Ellis-esque. The cocktails are stunning (Champagne Julep comes highly recommended) and the happy hour from 5pm-7pm brings the damage down to vaguely heart-attack defying

Oxygen
3-5 Infirmary Street (0131) 557 9997
Originally founded on the gimmick of canisters of fresh gas for that natural high, this gastro pub now concentrates on its very good food, a fine line up of DJs, imported beers and trendy cocktails – all of which it does pretty damned well. Ambient and friendly, this bar tends to attract a diverse crowd of students, older academics and professional drinkers – that's drinkers who are professionals, not people who drink for a living. Oh, and there's a nice little room downstairs that is ideal for parties.

levels. Sprawling rooms and low-slung seating lend the place an air of luxurious glamour in which to knock back a few classy beverages, pretend you're independently wealthy, keep a house in Monaco and know that Lady Victoria. Champagne socialism comes to rest in Edinburgh.
Mon-Sun 12pm-3am. Food: 12pm-10pm (reservations only). Rec. dish: Bento box £8.95, House Wine: £11.95

Outhouse
12a Broughton St Lane (0131) 557 6668
So chilled out it's semi-comatose, the Outhouse offers up old comfy seating, a massive beer garden and seasonal BBQs to well, just about anyone in the game for a bit of low key fun. You won't find many of your poser crowd in here, what you will find are a funky collection of laid back types hustling for pool, thrashing each other at table football and chatting up the bar staff. This is a fine place to waste away a weekend.
Mon-Sun 11am-1am. Happy Hour: Mon-Sun 4pm-7pm. Food: Mon-Thu 12pm-8pm, Fri-Sun 12pm-4pm. Rec. dish: Homemade grilled burgers from £4.30, House Wine: £8.50

Mon-Sun 10am-1am. No happy hour but student deals 2pm-5pm Mon-Thu and Silvercard obtained from www.oxygen-edinburgh.co.uk gets discounts 2pm-5pm Mon-Fri. Food: daily 11am-9pm. Rec. dish: Smoked haddock risotto £7.95, House Wine: £9.50

Pivo Caffe
2 Calton Road (0131) 557 2925

Why bother going to Prague, with its fancy Charles Bridge and exotic Eastern European women standing outside the McDonalds in Wenceslas Square offering you a good night or those mad cellar bars which open all night, until no one can even say their own name, when you can come here? This Czech theme bar, hiding at the foot of Calton hill is relaxed, friendly and (dare I say it?) authentic. Pivo, cerveja, bière, beer... whatever you call it, this is the place to get it.

Mon-Sun 4pm-3am. No happy hour but discounts with card obtained from bar
No food, House Wine: £5.70

Pop Rokit
3 Picardy Place (0131) 556 4272

Too cool for school. The steps downstairs look like a runway and the toilets aren't properly labelled, so it must be, like, the hippest place in town. This eccentric chrome wonderland serves top-notch G&Ts to a background of hip DJ beats. The chances of finding a seat to sink into are about as likely as waking up tomorrow and realising you're married to Kylie, and the queues for the bar are like Sainsbury's at Christmas. Add to that the whole 'which toilet's which' issue and you might find you need sedation before you can truly enjoy a night out here. We recommend a mixture of vodka and over the counter sleeping pills... you'll be fine.

Mon-Sun 11am-1am. Happy Hour: Mon-Fri 4pm-7pm Tenants, Best £1.50, house spirits & mixer £1.50. No admission cost.
Food: Mon-Sun 12pm-7pm. Rec. dish: All day breakfast £3.15, House Wine: £10

(i) Recommended

Hangover Breakfasts
- Bar:Alba
- Biblos
- City Café
- EH1
- Native State

Ricks
55a Frederick Street (0131) 622 7800

This is the kind of place where you need to be pissed when you get the bill – if your eyes can even half focus on the pound signs you'll definitely start crying. Swan on in in your business suit to rub shoulders with flash office workers and couples engaging in quiet tête-à-têtes. Laugh when they have to leave after a fight over who decided to order that expensive wine. Not a place for drinking yourself

under the table on cheap vodka, although it could probably make for a more enjoyable night, but sometimes you have to show some maturity – tone it down you lot before you put us to shame.

Mon-Sun 7am-1am. Food: Sun-Thu 7am-10pm, Fri-Sat 7am-11pm. Rec. dish: Coconut and basil chicken with steamed rice £6.45, House Wine: £12.15

Siglo
184 Cowgate (0131) 240 2850

This 'fun' pub is well, just sooo much fun. The poster paint décor is painfully bright, the crowd are always terrifyingly drunk and if you manage to leave without joining some kind of conga, 80s pop sing-a-long or being asked to get your tits out by a bloke in a purple wig you'll be lucky. Freshers, freaks and the young and foolish can't get enough of this place and the cash machine by the bar makes sure it's hard for them to leave. If Siglo was a cult you'd probably join it by mistake.

Mon-Sat 12pm-1am, Sun 12.30pm-1am
Happy Hour: 5pm-8pm, all day Wed/Sun
Food: Mon-Sat 12pm-9pm, Sun 12.30pm-9pm. Rec. dish: Haggis £3.45,
House Wine: £5.70

time to get out more?

The Three Sisters
139 Cowgate (0131) 622 6800
These three siblings have the Cowgate in the palm of their hands and rightly so. It's huge (with an equally sizeable beer garden to boot) but never feels too empty. How, we're not quite sure, but they manage to pull 'em in for pints and promos all year round. You're looking at a student, good time kinda crowd so leave your polite chit-chat at home and be prepared for a ruck at the bar. The Three Sisters are a guaranteed good night out and you won't even have to pay their taxi fare home.
Mon-Sun 9am-1am. Food: Mon-Sun 9am-9pm. Rec. dish: Chicken stuffed with haggis £6.45, House Wine: £9.95

Tonic
34a North Castle Street (0131) 225 6431
If your idea of a night on the cocktails is an unfortunate Tom Cruise wannabe spilling cheap shcnapps and getting random girls to snog each other for free Baileys, you've been spending too much time in the Med. At Tonic you'll find the classy approach to mixed up drinks fits the bill for any special

occasion. Refined, swanky and good value when you consider the large measures and premium spirits, this is somewhere to impress or be impressed. Bring a hot date and work your way through the paperback-sized menu – if you don't get to first base after taking someone here you really are a total failure.

Mon-Sun 3pm-1am, House Wine: £10.75

The Tron
9 Hunters Sq (0131) 226 0931

Not the classiest of joints but great for a cheap pint, a game of pool and some hang-over food. Also a popular place to catch most major sporting events on the big screen. This extremely colourful multi-level venue mainly attracts students and is also a great rendezvous for backpackers – you can always be sure to befriend/make enemies with an Aussie at the bar. Weekend nights downstairs can turn into quite a sweat pit unless you and your mates grab one of the more intimate alcoves furnished with big comfy sofas; easy to fall into, impossible to get out of.

Mon-Sat 11.30am-1am, Sun 12.30pm-1am
Food: Mon-Sun 12pm-7pm. Rec. dish: Cajun chicken panini £4.25, House Wine: £7.70

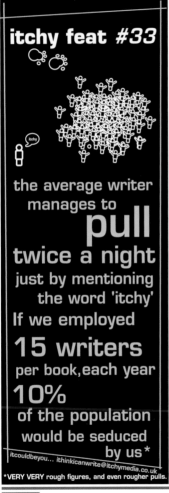
Uluru
133 Lothian Road (0131) 228 5407
Named after the outback's famous mono-lith, Uluru is for those who like to drink Australian. Fortunately the theme side to this bar is played down so you can actually enjoy a relaxing drink or quick game of pool without being confronted by crap kangaroo memorabilia everywhere you look. Bonza.
Mon-Sun 11am-1am. Food: Mon-Sun 12pm-7pm. Rec. dish: Paninis £4.25, House Wine: £5

Victoria & Albert
Frederick Street (0131) 226 4562
Describing itself as a pub and dining room, the V&A recently came over all classy. Edinburgh's revamped bars tend to be a bit hit and miss, but this one makes the grade. Classy and chic with leather seats and glass topped tables – no clandestine games of footsie here – this is somewhere worth putting on your night out radar. It's becoming a firm favourite with us.
Mon-Sat 12pm-1am, Sun 12pm-12.30am
Happy Hour: 5.30pm-7pm bottles 2-4-1.
Food: 12pm-10pm. Rec. dish: Lamb burger £7.50, House Wine: £11 (£6 Happy Hour)

Wash
11 North Bank Street (0131) 225 6193
70s retro like it should be. Wash manages to put the tasteful into 70s décor and if you

don't believe us, you'll have to go and check it out yourself. Looking down on Princes Street like an aloof club bouncer and offering wickedly garish cocktails, this is somewhere to forget any vague concept of cool and get down like flares and afros never went out of fashion.

Mon-Sat 12pm-1am, Sun 12.30pm-1am
Happy Hour: Mon-Sun 4pm-8pm 2-4-1
Food: Mon-Sun 12pm-7pm. Rec. dish:
Nachos £5, House Wine: £7.50

Yo!Below
66 Rose Street (0131) 220 6040

A modern Japanese eating and drinking experience at its gadgety best. Manga films are projected onto the walls, beer flows from taps on the tables and, in between dishing up plates of sushi and steaming noodles, the waiting staff belt out karaoke classics with debateable talent. Wanna hear more? How about expert tarot readers to predict your destiny and an at-table massage service? Cool, slick and undeniably kitsch, Yo!Below is a firm favourite with itchy HQ.

Sun-Fri 5pm-1am, Sat 12pm-1am
Happy Hour: 6pm-8pm every day 2-4-1
selected beer and house wine. Food: 5pm-11pm. Rec. dish: Beef ramen £6.50
House Wine: £11

pubs

www.itchyedinburgh.co.uk

Aubrey's Bar
2b Jamaica Street (0131) 476 5333
Owned and run by the affable Aubrey Price, this boozer is so well hidden that if you blink you miss it. It's worth seeking out though, especially at weekends when the pokey venue becomes a crazed bacchanalian den of sin straight out of National Lampoon's Animal House. Despite its size there are two floors and bars on offer and some cosy, scarlet interior design. The wall-of-shame photos behind the bar are worth a laugh.
Mon-Sun 12pm-1am
(No food as we went to press but a refurb is on the cards)

Bannermans
121 Cowgate (0131) 556 3254
The old man's boozer exterior belies a lively young whippersnapper of a pub on the inside. In case you haven't put two and two together yet, yep we're talking another student favourite. And keeping the city's job dodgers away from lectures is no problem at Bannerman's – beer: check, gigs: check, WWF on TV: check – those crazy student types are in their element.
Mon-Sat 12pm-1am, Sun 12.30pm-1am
Food: Mon-Thu 5pm-10pm, Fri-Sat 12pm-10pm, Sun 12.30pm-4pm & 5pm-10pm

Beehive
18-20 Grassmarket (0131) 225 7171
The Beehive's proximity to crowd magnets Espionage and the Three Sisters has miraculously not effected its popularity. They've managed to corner the older market and there's no messing around on the décor front either. Rather than using the 'just cram it full of fake old stuff and hope for the best' method of Edinburgh boozer design, they've kept things simple and effective. For a quiet midweek catch up session or mid-afternoon skive, the Beehive is well worth a visit. Just watch out for Aunty Doris's 40th birthday bash at the weekend disco nights.
Mon-Sun 11.30am-1am
Food: 11.30am-10pm

Bennets Bar
8 Leven Street (0131) 229 5143
Bennets Bar is the quintessential old man's pub. And, like all quintessential old men's pubs in the centre of Edinburgh, it has been invaded by students. The old-fashioned décor, ornate benches and heavy mirrors give this place a local-pub-in-an-English-pit-town feel. Unpretentious, smoky and relaxed, Bennets is a great venue for whiling away a wet Sunday afternoon in front of the rugby.
Mon-Sat 11am-12.30am
Sun 12.30pm-12.30am
Food: Mon-Sat 12pm-2pm & 5pm-8.30pm

Biddy Mulligans
96 Grassmarket (0131) 220 1246
If you fancy joining a quick verse of 'The Irish Rover' or indulging in a bit of table dancing

(not in that way you perverts) then this is the place for you. Drawing the crowds from the heart of the city, Biddy Mulligans dark and dingy décor is brightened by its good time customers; from the wandering tourist to the student hordes, here you'll find the best atmosphere outside Murrayfield on match day.
Mon-Sun 9am-1am
Food: Mon-Sun 9am-9pm

Black Bull
12 Grassmarket (0131) 225 6636
For those times when even the slightest hint of cool is going to do your head in, this place is midweek pints, big screen footie and no messing all the way. Roll up for bog standard pub grub and decent ale. Stags and hens invade at weekends, bringing with them their own unique brand of style and glamour. Check out the face on the mother-in-law to be as the bridesmaid recounts tales of her and the bride simulating sex on a podium in Magaluf. Scary stuff.
Mon-Thu 11am-12am, Fri-Sat 11am-1am,
Sun 12.30pm-12am
Food: Mon-Sat 11am-10pm,
Sun 12.30pm-10pm

The Blind Poet
32c West Nicholson St (0131) 667 0876

This is one of those pubs that manages to make you feel more bohemian intellectual than sad old alcoholic – something that can't be underestimated as far as we're concerned. Rock up here for an afternoon's liver-pickling, and before you know it you and your mates have devised a screen-play idea and invented a new kind of wheel. There'll be no slipping shots into your flatmate's lager and trying to take his pants off in here you know...

Mon-Sun 11am-1am

Cloisters
26 Brougham Street (0131) 221 9997

Forgive me father for I am about to sin... It might seem a little unholy to be downing alcopops in an old church but if a little something like that's going to put you off... Back with us are you? Good. You'll find this a friendly, cosy kind of place, somewhere to bag a seat by the fire and settle in for a long winter's evening. Despite its holy background Cloisters feels like somewhere where you could get into loads of trouble.

Mon-Thu 11am-12am, Fri-Sat 11am-12.30am, Sun 11am-12am. Food: Mon-Fri 12pm-3pm, Sat-Sun 12pm-4pm

Finnegan's Wake
9b Victoria Street (0131) 226 3816

Okay, so Irish theme pubs are ten a penny, but if you're up for a night of sheer drunken revelry, then do yourself a favour and visit Finnegan's. With live bands playing a mixture of traditional Irish tunes alongside covers of more popular hits seven nights a week this place is always jumping. The queues may be long, seats may be scarce, but after your umpteenth Guinness you won't give a damn. Friendly service, averagely priced drinks and a high percentage of fine looking Irish lads and lasses means Finnegan's never fails to deliver that Celtic good time package.

Mon-Sun 1pm-1am

(i) **Recommended**

Watch The Football
- Bannerman's
- Mather's
- The Tron

Greyfriar's Bobby
34 Candlemaker Row (0131) 225 8328

Named after that little yappy fella who took his status as man's best friend a little too seriously, this pub is stuffed full of dog memorabilia and yep, you've guessed it, students. A traditional comfy boozer with food and drink at overdraft friendly prices, Greyfriar's may not make much of a springboard to a wild night out but it makes a change from style bar hell. The dog's bollocks? Not quite, but we're loving this place for a Sunday afternoon pint.
Mon-Sun 11am-1am
Food: Mon-Sun 12pm-6.45pm

The Hogshead
20 Bread Street (0131) 221 0575
22 Castle Street (0131) 226 1224

Seen one Hogshead, seen 'em all. Read one of our Hogshead reviews, read them all. Here's the party-line: inoffensive (for the chain brigade), identikit boozers with decent beers on offer. There are beer festivals for ale anoraks and non-smoking areas for those who haven't yet discovered that smoking is cool. You could do a lot worse. But you sure as hell could do a lot better.
Mon-Sun 11am-1am
Food: Mon-Sun 12pm-8pm

Holyrood Tavern
9a Holyrood Road (0131) 556 5044

Not a theme in sight. Old without being 'ye olde', the Holyrood Tavern is a proper no-nonsense pub for proper no-nonsense people. They won't put your pint on a napkin and they won't bring it over to your table for you, but if they did, the majority of their clientele would probably walk out in shock anyway. A cracking pub quiz and a rock-tastic juke-box make this somewhere to get familiar with as soon as.
Mon-Sun 12pm-1am
Food: Mon-Sun 12pm-2pm & 5pm-8.30pm

Kings Bar
Bruntsfield Hotel, 69-74 Bruntsfield Pl. (0131) 229 1393

A bar fit for a King? Possibly. But then again, considering centuries of inbreeding have pretty much killed off any chance of a Royal genius would you trust their judgement? The Kings Bar tries – and fails – to be a little bit more than just a hotel bar. It's one of the few pubs in the Bruntsfield area that hasn't been taken over by the student population – perhaps, unlike their blue blooded rulers, they're not as stupid as they look?
Mon-Wed 11am-12.30am, Thu-Sat 11am-1am, Sun 12.30pm-1am
Food: Mon-Sun 12pm-9pm

The Malt Shovel
11-15 Cockburn Street (0131) 225 6843
Yer basic boozer, handily located round the corner from Waverly Station for that

pre/post-train pint. It's trip-over-the-piles-of-suitcases dark, but fairly busy all year round. Cheapskates will be in their element with bargain grub and a good value array of whiskies. Don't get too settled in though... there's that train to catch remember?
Mon-Thu 11am-12am, Fri-Sat 11am-1am,
Sun 12.30pm-12am. Food: Mon-Thu 12pm-
7pm, Fri 12pm-5pm, Sat-Sun 12pm-6pm

Mathers
25 Broughton Street (0131) 556 6754
Right in the heart of Broughton Street's trendy bars and cafés, sits this old man's boozer. Mathers has staunchly refused to make any concessions to the modern age (well, apart from electric lighting and indoor toilets) and is all the better for it. A great place to enjoy a pint in front of the footie and eavesdrop on conversations about how young people don't know they're born.
Mon-Thu 11am-12am, Fri-Sat 11am-
12.30am, Sun 12.30pm-12am
Food: Mon-Sun 12pm-8pm

Pear Tree House
38 West Nicolson Street (0131) 667 7533
Most of the pubs round these parts have upgraded in honour of the student rent-a-crowds, but the Pear Tree has stuck to its guns and shunned the revamp concept completely. The huge beer garden makes it a busy festival hangout, while the daily pile-it-high buffet and coal fire ensure that the ravages of winter are easily ignored. Don't mess with the staff though, last time we were in they didn't take too kindly to our 'hilarious' drunken banter. It seems challenging them to a drunken arm wrestle isn't quite their idea of fun.
Mon-Thu 11am-12am, Fri-Sat 11am-1am,
Sun 12.30pm-12am
Food: Mon-Fri 12pm-3pm

Penny Black
14 West Register Street (0131) 556 1106
Tucked away in an alley off Princes Street this odd little boozer's unusual opening hours have carved an unsurprising niche in the 'it's 5am and I'm gagging for a pint' market. If you regularly visit this establishment

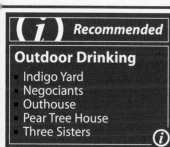

Recommended

Outdoor Drinking

- Indigo Yard
- Negociants
- Outhouse
- Pear Tree House
- Three Sisters

chances are you're either a night-shift worker, a student or have an embryonic drink problem. Combine a pounding morning-after head with an apparent inability to drink more than 3mm of your pint in one sip and you're suffering from a nasty bout of what has come to be known in the city's medical circles as P.B.S (Penny Black Syndrome).

Mon-Sun 5am-11pm. No food

Rose Street Brewery
55-57 Rose Street (0131) 220 1227
The name of this pub leaves very little to the imagination... it is a Brewery and it is indeed on Rose Street. Very much in keeping with the Rose Street traditional pub ethos, the place is decked out in dark panelling with leather benches and walls full of auld Edinburgh prints. If your interest in beer goes beyond just drinking it, you can take a quick tour of the on-premises brewery. Take this opportunity to prove you can organise a piss-up in one...
Mon-Sat 11am-1am, Sun 12.30pm-11pm
Food: Mon-Sun 12pm-9pm

The Southsider
3 West Richmond Street (0131) 667 2003
It appears last year's makeover wasn't meant to be. They've done away with the trendy colour scheme and fancy furnishings and gone back to basics in an old skool pub style. You could be forgiven for thinking this must be where all the old men come now all their haunts have turned into wanky style bars, but you're more likely to find it full of pissed-up students than pensioners supping a Guinness. For table football or a game of pool you've just struck gold, otherwise we're not so sure. The service in here was dire on our last visit, but they could have just taken a particular dislike to us – they wouldn't be the first – but we get the feeling that everyone suffers the same.
Mon-Thu 11am-12am, Fri-Sat 11am-1am, Sun 12pm-12am
Food: Mon-Sun 12pm-2.30pm & 6pm-9pm

itchy feat #40

itchy send out over **5000**
SMS messages a day [VIP club entry, FREE beer etc]
If all the beeps were put in a jar
then opened on a sunny day

the resulting **BEEP**
would be 10 times louder
than a **Jumbo Jet** taking off,
and would probably blow you up*.

*absolute rubbish

Standing Order
62-66 George Street (0131) 225 4460
Once a bank, now a boozer, the Standing Order occupies one of many prestigious George Street buildings. The columns and high ceilings cannot, however, make up for the effect of the Wetherspoons touch that successfully decimates any initial potential for style or atmosphere. This vast, music-less and excessively smoky drinking hall is decked with fruit machines and standard, drab pub furniture and carpets. One can only suggest that the large crowds it attracts are the result of its central location and cheap drinks (a 2 pint pitcher for a mere

£3.19). If you want a night out that won't send you over your overdraft limit then Wetherspoons is the answer, but wouldn't it be worth paying a little extra and going somewhere good?
Mon-Sat 10am-1am, Sun 12.30pm-1am
Food: Mon-Sun 10am-10pm

Ye Olde Golf Tavern
30 Wright's Houses (0131) 229 1093
Ye Olde Golf Tavern sits just on the edge of ye olde Bruntsfield Links. Believe it or not this pub might have a golf theme but it isn't as tacky as it sounds. The Golf is unpretentious yet original, and attracts a mix of locals, students, young professionals and families. For lazy Sunday afternoons, a pub feed, evening drinks or a post pitch and putt pint (you can hire golf clubs from behind the bar to use on the Links) you could do a lot worse.
Mon-Sun 11am-1am. Food: Mon-Thu 11am-7pm, Fri-Sat 11am-7pm (snack menu) 7pm- 9pm, Sun 11am-7pm

clubs

www.itchyedinburgh.co.uk

Beat Jazz Basement
1a Chambers Street (0131) 467 2539

A small neon sign on Chambers Street depicting the Blue Note Jazz label signals the entrance to a new venue built on the ashes of the much lamented (by us anyway), Cellar Bar. Furthermore, it echoes the music policy of the much more widely lamented, Café Graffiti, particularly in its eclecticism. More traditional vocal jazz earlier in the week gives way to a weirder, but no less brilliant, experimental jazz as the week progresses. There's a genuine buzz of excitement from the collective masses when the lights go down and the band (or collective or whatever) strikes up. Add to this the minimal lighting behind the bar and the candle on each table which create a sultry atmosphere and you have one fine venue.

Berties
7 Merchant Street (0131) 225 2002

I don't know who Bertie is, but I think I can imagine... Late 40s (still trying to pass for 30), bit of a lard arse (considering a Captain Kirk girdle), would wear a gold chain if his chest was hairy enough and has a penchant for young girls. He's cheap, open all hours and decidedly more attractive after a bottle of vodka. But girl's, if you're tempted, you're sure to regret it the morning after.

The Bongo Club
14 New Street (off the Canongate)
(0131) 556 5204

The Bongo club values substance over style. With live music and club nights covering ska and dub reggae to African, Latin and Caribe (Arakataca) or hip hop, funk and house (Headspin), this club corners the market on alternative beats. As multi-purpose as a Black and Decker drill, by day the Bongo Club transforms into a café and exhibition space playing host to a random selection of classes – possibly the best place in Scotland for a little djembe drumming.

Cabaret Voltaire
36-38 Blair Street (0131) 220 6176

Formerly the Peppermint Lounge, this is now home to a truly eclectic – a word we use far too freely, but we really mean it here – venue. The name Cabaret Voltaire stems from the Dada movement which was born in 1916. The aim was to cure the madness of the age through art. So what's this got to do with 21st Century clubbing? Not a great deal really, but in a time when the club scene has become rather predictable and stale the people behind Cabaret Voltaire, Freak Marketing, are aiming to give the capital's club scene a much-needed kick up the arse. Nights range from live acoustic music, classic hip hop breaks with R'n'B through to nu skool breaks and D'n'B. On top of this they aim to encourage people to congregate, socialise and network through the exhibition space, workshop and club that are housed within. So is this is the future for the clubbing world or just a preposterously pretentious gamble? Get down their yourself and make up your own mind up.

Cavendish
West Tollcross (0131) 228 3252

Cavendish purports to promote an over-25 policy, whether this works or not is open to question. More likely this is an honest concession to the fact that the punters inside are just as out of date as the club itself. Expect 80s and 90s 'classics', but the only similarity to Skool Disco is the fact that most of the punters will be dancing like your old cardigan clad physics teacher.

CC Blooms
23 Greenside Place (0131) 556 9331

Handbags at the ready. CC's is Edinburgh's only gay club. A popular and happy little haunt, with mirrored walls to make it feel a little bigger but it doesn't stop the sweat dripping from the ceiling as the camp customers enjoy the nightly diet of hi-energy disco and house classics. They say size isn't everything and it's what you do with it that counts and, although no doubt a lot of the punters here would disagree, when it's in club form it's certainly true.

Citrus Club
38-40 Grindlay Street (0131) 622 7086

"Here we are now. Entertain us". The Citrus Club answered Kurt Cobain's call and years later it still dishes out tormented tunes to its underdressed and under washed audience. Ok, so four years spent lying amongst pizza boxes and empty beer cans in that student bed sit in Tollcross wasn't all that bad – but do you really want to relive it now? Maybe this club owes its success to the short-term memory damage that most of its punters seem to have suffered. Smells like Teen Spirit? Plain reeks of Merrydown and spesh more like.

Club Java
Commercial Street, Leith (0131) 467 3810

Worth the trek to Leith. Another recently converted church – it's hard to believe that the God fearing folk of Edinburgh can rock up anywhere on Sunday without finding out it's turned into the latest McTheme bar – Java attracts the slightly more discerning clubber who opts for savvy beats over S Club. The last Saturday of every month sees 'Oxygen' breathe some life into funky house courtesy of resident DJ Alpha and guests. Also worth noting is that 'Oxygen' operate a free taxi service where five paying customers can claim back up to £4 at the door with a valid taxi receipt.

Club Mercado
36-39 Market Street (0131) 226 4224

Nine-to-five central, you'd think somewhere as tacky as this would have been shaken off long ago. But, like that little lump of chewing gum on the bottom of your shoe, it just won't go away and it gathers crap as time wears on. Club Mercado thrives so much on tack it's a wonder they haven't changed the name to Super Mercado. Bright colours, bouncy people, cheesy chart tunes and never a bad night out. It might not be the height of sophistication but Brenda loves it.

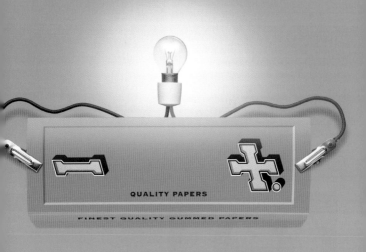

QUALITY PAPERS

FINEST QUALITY GUMMED PAPERS

ww.rizla.com RIZLA + **It's what you make of it.**

Ego
14 Picardy Place (0131) 478 7434

Where do you start with this place? You could bang on about Freud and psychoanalysis if you wanted to look like a smart arse, but you'd eventually get round to fancying your own mum, which is just plain not right, so forget that. Instead we should focus on the array of legendary club nights on offer, such as 'Joy' on Saturdays which is the best trance and hard house night in the city with a gay-friendly crowd or the guest appearances by the likes of Mr Scruff. Then we should mention the decadent interior with burgundy-coloured walls sporting huge Renaissance-style paintings and the numerous mirrorballs suspending from the ceiling. Finally, we should mention, if you haven't guessed already, that we like this place and suggest you get yourself down here sharpish.

appealing than spending an evening fight-ing your way through hordes of today's you dressed head-to-toe in Topman/shop an tanked up on alcopops. This club is big, wit a capacity of 2100 spread over two danc floors – there is scope for improvement her but it fails to deliver. Although the night vary with regard to music policy and entr fees the only consistent factor throughout that the drinks are served lukewarm b grouchy staff and the overall vibe is so bad hurts. Perfect if you're 30 going on 16 and u for a fumble with a pre-pubescent la soaked in his dad's aftershave.

Eros & Elite
Fountainspark, Dundee Street
(0131) 228 1661

Saturday night at home with Matthew Kelly and a family pack of Doritos is far more

Espionage
Victoria Street (0131) 477 7007

The only thing you're likely to spy Espionage is Billy the Bank Manager wrap ping his tongue round Sheila th Supermarket Girl's tonsils. 007 liked it sha en not stirred, dear old Sheila likes hers ra

Forget the house scene

ed and banged. There's more levels than Cher's had face-lifts, free entry, a door that stays open 'til three and a dancefloor that's always rammed. They say you get what you pay for, and reap what you sow – Sheila, your mother didn't say "shut it" for nothing.

Establishment
Semple Street (0131) 229 7733

This club, formally known as The Arc, has had a bit of an image makeover. As we went to press the doors had just reopened on this lounge-bar-style club. Although it's early days, Establishment's trendy new look and DJ line-up have already started to pack the punters in. For updates see www.itchyedinburgh.co.uk.

Gaia
8 Kings Stable Road (0131) 229 9438

Gaia is home to 'Shagtag', Edinburgh's lonely hearts clubbing made simple. None of your SOH and walks in the dales bollocks, the atmosphere here is hot and sweaty – but

that could be more to do with the lack of air conditioning. Just off the Grassmarket this is a popular student haunt and dirt cheap drinks prices ensure they keep coming back for more. The music policy is pure cheese, so there's plenty of Tiffany and Rick Astley on offer. On Mondays, 'Tentastic' is ten quid in and then free drinks all night – liver transplants are not covered in the entry fee.

Henry's Jazz Cellar
8 Morrison Street (0131) 567 5200

It's dark, smoky and frankly disgusting, but it's also wonderful. Henry's captures all that is right about jazz and encapsulates it in a basic basement bar. Naturally, it's a big favourite with 'aren't I so cool?' art students, but they are easily ignored as you tuck into another reasonably priced Budvar and get lost in the eclectic mix of live jazz. Be warned though – it's extremely popular at weekends, so get there early to grab a seat.

La Belle Angele
11 Hastie's Close (0131) 225 7536

Dark, dingy and definitely no fromage, La Belle is grass roots Edinburgh at its best. There might be nothing flashy or plush about this place, but the atmosphere is friendly and the punters are chilled out. Clubbing for people who do what they like and like what they do, this wee beauty showcases some of the best nights in Auld Reekie. Each month on Fridays it plays host to Manga – one of the greatest D'n'B nights in the land. It's crazy and dirty so why aren't you there already?

Get out more in the all-new Ford**Fiesta**

The Liquid Room
79c Victoria Street (0131) 225 2564

A hop, skip and a jump from th
Grassmarket. Expect to queue, but re
assured that the wait is well worth it – dor
make the dreadful mistake of going int
neighbouring Espionage because there's r
queue for it – there's a good reason for tha
After bumping down the stairs on your ars
(perhaps that last tequila slammer was
bad idea?) you'll stumble into a gem of
club. There's a thundering sound system ar
plenty of room to throw some shapes.
popular venue with students taking adva
tage of the cheap drinks promotio
through the week, the more serious clu
bers strut their funky stuff at the weekenc
when the venue plays host to various gue
DJs from near and far. The interior could
with a bit of spit and polish but it's in kee
ing with the deep down and dirty groove
Expect a crowd who are out to enjoy ther
selves as much as you are.

Potterrow
Bristo Place (0131) 650 9195

Edinburgh University's student union
worth a mention because, in a city of cel
clubs, it's one of the largest central venue
Still, it is well and truly a union, with che
drinks, drunk students and, like all jo

...odger joints, the bar staff are pretty decent
... and in a city like Edinburgh, with so many
...ack-handed baboons behind the bar, that is
...o bad thing. Yeah, like you'd expect, they
...am out the post-chart classics by the trolley
...oad, but there's a lot more to Potterow than
...our clichéd university offering... they also
...ttract some tasty acts from DJs to live
...ands. Worthy of your student loan.

Po Na Na
3b Frederick Street (0131) 226 2224

Revolution
31 Lothian Road (0131) 229 7670

The Revolution will not be televised... and it
certainly won't take place on Lothian Road.
This is not what Marx, Lenin and Mao were
striving for, but it suits Marie, Leah and Marty
just fine. This is the kind of club you'd expect
to find housed within some cheap hotel in
Liverpool. Take one crumbling old cinema-
building, fill with glitter balls, tacky lighting
effects, paltry sound system and swarms of
"mad fer it" townies. There, now you have
your very own Revolution.

Studio 24
Calton Road (0131) 558 3758

Don't be put off by the Desperate Dan look-
a-likes on the door, Studio 24 is a must for

...o matter how hard we try to avoid it we
...sually seem to end up here at the end of
...e night, and we always seem to have a
...ood time – as far as I remember. Decorated
... a fez-tastic manner, Po Na Na has spread
...rough the UK faster than an outbreak of
...oot-and-mouth disease. Expect what you
...und in the same club in Manchester,
...ambridge, Sheffield and so on, which basi-
...ally boils down to good tunes, chilled areas
...nd a fairly hefty array of booze.

those who like their music hard whatever
the genre. For some reason this club is trying
to pull a hard house and gothic rock crowd
and for some reason it's succeeding. The
sound system will rock you to your core
which may explain why this club is rammed
weekend in and weekend out. What it does-
n't explain is how on earth so many badly-
dressed people have managed to all fit into
one building without the fashion police
coming along and closing it down.

Subway
Cowgate (0131) 225 6766

For years scientists have searched for the Missing Link, and then, one Friday night in Subway, the mystery was solved. The name Subway conjures up images of underground (read: übercool) beats; unfortunately the reality is more under life (read: townie) freaks. Students are meant to be educated but, after a bottle of 20/20, they still seem to end up here by the truckload. Fuelled by cheap alcopops and even cheaper choons. The punters have it large and regret it massively every night of the week in this poptastic pit. A place where the drinks prices are truly as low as the punters.

Subway West End
Lothian Road (0131) 229 9197

The first mistake to make when trying to dis-associate a club from Subway is to include Subway in the name. Teeming with blue collar lads and lassies wantin' to go pure off their heeds and o' that. The amount of intelligent conversation runs into the negative. Quite literally the only taste offered here is last night's dinner on the back of punters' tonsils. Frankly, Subway West End is bollocks, and a sweaty pair at that. Have we given you enough reasons not to go there? Right then, moving swiftly on...

The Venue
Calton Road (0131) 557 3073

Warning to all ladies visting here: make sur you take a leak before you enter, and needs be, don't drink pints when you'r inside. You really do not want to be visitin the toilets here. The floor is sodden at a times, but the lack of loo seat means yo have to employ the hover technique. Ok that said, the Venue is well worth a visit. It had an impessive sound system installec there's almost always a friendly crowd insid and the DJs have some of the most eclecti playlists in town. Who needs toilets anyway

Why Not?
14 George Street (0131) 624 8633

For those wot speak with plums in the mouths, or at least have an HND in accoun ancy. Why Not? attracts an aspiring 20 something crowd of wannabe somebody somedays from Standard Life and the lik Gold cards at the ready and don't worry you picked yours up at the airport – you'll f right in. Always worth popping down to se how the other half behave before they settl down to a life of conformity, mundanity, 2 kids and three pints of semi every day. Wh not? Because it's arse, that's why.

BECK'S

BRAUEREI BECK & CO.
BECK'S
BIER BEER
BREMEN · GERMANY

JUGGLER
(APPRENTICE)

club listings

For up-to-date listings, reviews and previews go to www.itchyedinburgh.co.uk

All listings details are liable to change at short notice and should therefore be used as a guide only

Night	Music	Price	Closes	Notes
MONDAY				
CC Blooms	Chart	Free	3am	No dress code, gay club
Vod:bull @ Liquid Room	Funk, hip hop, R'n'B	£4	3am	No dress code, student night
Acoustica @ Cabaret Voltaire	Live acoustic	Free		Voluntary donations. No covers - it's not Stars In Your Eyes
Groove Bonanza @ Po Na Na	Disco, house, party	Free	3am	No dress code
Decadence @ Revolution	Chart	£4, £2 NUS	3am	No dress code, student night
Subway	Indie	£3/£1	3am	Check for dress code
TUESDAY				
CC Blooms	Chart	Free	3am	No dress code, gay club
Vibe @ Ego	Dance	£2	3am	Check for dress code, gay night
Shagtag @ Gaia	Cheese, dance	£4, £2 discount	3am	Check for dress code
Yerba Buena @ Po Na Na	Salsa, Latin	Free (fee for class)	3am	No dress code
Wax-Factor @ Liquid Room	Breaks, hip hop, funk	Free	3am	No dress code
Subway	Indie	£3/£1	3am	Check for dress code
WEDNESDAY				
CC Blooms	Chart	Free	3am	No dress code, gay club
Planet @ The Cavendish	Cheese	£3, £2 NUS	3am	No dress code, student night
Slap & Tickle @ Club Mercado	Funk	Free with Snap fax b4 10.30pm, £1 b4 11.30pm £4, £3 guest list	3am	Smart/sexy dress code
M2K/Traffic Light Night @ Gaia	Alt. indie, disco	£4, £3/£2 discount	3am	Check for dress code, student night
Low Gravity @ Liquid Room	Nu-breaks, hip hop	£3, £2 discount	3am	No dress code
BBJD/Bootylicious @ Cabaret V	Soulful R'n'B, hip hop	£4		£1 donation to charity per student
Bling @ Po Na Na	R'n'B, hip hop	£4/£3 NUS	3am	Smart/casual dress code
Pop Idols @ Revolution	Karaoke	£4, £2 discount	3am	Check for dress code
Kero-Scene-K2 @ Studio 24	Metal	£1.50	3am	No dress code
Subway	Indie	£3/£1	3am	Check for dress code, student night
THURSDAY				
CC Blooms	Chart	Free	3am	No dress code, gay club
Chango @ Cabaret Voltaire	World music, D'n'B	£4		Weekly guest DJs
Thursdays In The City @ Club Mercado	Party	Free	3am	Check for dress code
Sin @ Eros/Elite	Party	£3	3am	Check for dress code
Opium	Rock, nu-metal & alternative, indie	Free	3am	Check for dress code
Snatch Club @ Liquid Room	Funk, hip hop	£3.50, £2.50 discount	3am	No dress code
TLC @ Po Na Na	Hip hop, R'n'B, pop	£4/£3 NUS	3am	Smart/casual dress code
Old Skool Disco @ Revolution	Retro house	£4, £2 NUS	3am	School uniform essential
Subway	Indie	£3/£1	3am	Check for dress code, student night

Night	Music	Price	Closes	Notes
FRIDAY				
CC Blooms	Chart	Free	3am	No dress code, gay club
Mardi Gras @ The Cavendish	70s-modern day	£6	3am	Check for dress code, over 25s only
Planet Earth @ The Citrus Club	80s	£4	3am	Check for dress code
Time Tunnel/4 Play @ Club Mercado	Funk/chart, cheese & dance	£5 & £4 with flyer for Time Tunnel, Free for 4 Play	4am	Smart but casual dress code
Lush @ Eros/Elite	Party	£6, £5 b4 12 free b4 10pm	3am	Check for dress code, over 19s only
Canned Heat @ Gaia	R'n'B, hip hop, pop	£2 b4 12, £4 after	3am	No dress code
Opium	Rock, nu-metal & alternative, indie	Free	3am	Check for dress code
Evol @ Liquid Room	Indie	£4	3am	No dress code
Roadblock @ Po Na Na	80s classics	Free b4 11pm, £4 11pm-12am, £5 after 12am	3am	Smart/casual dress code
Ibiza Foam Party @ Revolution	House, garage	Check venue	3am	Check for dress code
Subway	Indie	£3/£1	3am	Check for dress code, student night
Cabaret Voltaire	Global, jazz, dancehall	£5-£9 varies each week		Weekly rotation so call for more info
SATURDAY				
CC Blooms	Chart	Free	3am	No dress code, gay club
Saturday Sensation @ The Cavendish	70s, 80s, 90s	£6	3am	Check for dress code, over 25s only
Tease Age @ The Citrus Club	Indie, big beat, soul & funk	£4	3am	Check for dress code
Heaven @ Eros/Elite	Party	Prive varies	3am	Check for dress code, over 20s only
Opium	Rock, nu-metal & alternative, indie	Free	3am	Check for dress code
Love Groove @ Gaia	70s to current chart	£2 b4 12, £4 after	3am	No dress code
Funky Sensual @ Po Na Na	Funky, soulful house	Same prices as Fri	3am	Smart but casual dress code
Supernova @ Revolution	Chart, party	£5, £3 b4 12	3am	Check for dress code
Subway	Indie	£3/£1	3am	Check for dress code, student night
Diggity @ The Establishment	R'n'B	£6, £5 with flyer	3am	Check for dress code
Popcorn/Ultragroove @ Cabaret Voltaire	Hip hop to soulful	£7-£10 depending on which week		Fortnightly rotations, call for more info
SUNDAY				
CC Blooms	Chart	Free	3am	No dress code, gay club
Pimp/HRT @ The Cavendish	R'n'B, hip hop/ party classics	£3, £2/£1 discount	3am	Check for dress code
Mode Organic @ The Citrus Club	Ska, soul, funk, mod & freakbeat	£2	3am	Check for dress code
Steppin Out @ Eros/Elite	Chart	Price varies	3am	Check for dress code, over 18s only
Taste @ Liquid Room	House, garage, funk	£8, £6 members	3am	Check for dress code
Live bands @ Po Na Na	Live funk	£3/£2 NUS	1am	No dress code
OKY @ Studio 24	Rock, goth, metal, industrial, punk	£2, £1.50 b4 12	3am	No dress code
Sin @ The Establishment	Cheese, pop	£2, £1 discount	3am	Check for dress code
Bass D Funk @ The Venue	Breakbeat, house, hip hop	£5, free b4 12	3am	Check for dress code
Escape from New York @ Caberet Voltaire	Electro soundtrack to artists' sculpting	Free entry, £2 to leave		Create your own sculptures and works of art. Materials provided

cafés

www.itchyedinburgh.co.uk

Beanscene
67 Holyrood Road (0131) 557 6549
99 Nicolson Street (0131) 667 8159

Less obvious than the other coffee chains, this is a cosy café popular with the loafing student posse. On a sunny weekend (don't scoff, we do have them) the windows slide open and there's not a spare chair in sight, making Beanscene feel more like an open house than a café. Drinks and food are quite expensive and not altogether inspiring, but their marshmallow and cream-laden hot chocolates are worth risking a heart attack for.

Mon-Sat 8am-10pm, Sun 10am-10pm
(Holyrood Road)
Mon-Sat 7.30am-10pm, Sun 10am-10pm
(Nicolson Street)

Black Medicine
2 Nicolson Street (0131) 622 7209

A few years old now but not showing any signs of decay, although the seats are still quite literally a pain in the arse. That said, very good coffee and a cracking line in fruit smoothies are probably worth the mild discomfort, so bring a cushion if the wooden seating worries you, you big girl's blouse.

Mon-Sat 8am-8pm, Sun 9am-8pm

Bookstop Café
4 Teviot Place (0131) 225 5298

Bookstop Café is the inverse of the plethora of little cafés springing up in bookshops across the country. A tiny little café with a small selection of seemingly randomly selected books (and a few for sale) so you can imagine you're an impoverished wordsmith on the verge of your first big advance cheque. A curious oddity and a firm favourite of the art student brigade it offers an interesting, albeit limited, selection of food and drink at not-so-large prices.
Mon-Sat 9am-6pm, Sun 10am-6pm

Cafe Florentin
10 Grassmarket (0131) 220 2242
8 St Giles Street (0131) 225 6267

Florentin's is a cosy, split-level café with long opening hours, which serves the kind of almondy, flaky patisserie God created on the eighth day and saved for himself. A hit with tourists and arty riff-raff alike, it's ideal for troughing croissants and posing over a copy of L'Etranger whilst pondering the Death of God. Well worth being patronised by a snotty waiter for – well, it's more French, non?
Mon-Sun 8am-6pm (until 4pm in winter)

Café Lucano
37-39 George IV Bridge (0131) 225 6690

Opposite the bustling Elephant House, and equally close to the uni, this place seems to have been bypassed by the student crowds, which is no bad thing really. The atmosphere is pretty laid back and there are a decent range of snacks and larger main courses, but

Café Lucano somehow lacks that secret ingredient which makes the rest of Edinburgh's cafes so addictive.
Mon-Fri 7am-10pm, Sat 8am-10pm
Sun 9am-8pm

California Coffee Co.
(0131) 228 5001
Buccleuch Street, Lauriston Place, Leith Street, Rose Street, St Patrick Square and other locations throughout Edinburgh.

These ex-police boxes dotted throughout the city serve up quality caffeine hits to people on the go (and many would argue they are more useful than in their previous incarnation). The staff are remarkably friendly considering they're stuck in a box whatever the weather with barely enough room to pick their noses let alone make a cappuccino.

Chocolate Soup
2 Hunter Square (0131) 225 7669

Chocolate soup? I don't know, young folk today will try anything...This café has earned a place in Edinburgh's heart for dishing out bowls of hot chocolate and appetising snacks. Not as cosy as it could be, but still a good bet for a city centre pit stop.
Mon-Sun 8am-6pm

the elephant house

21 George VI Bridge
0131 220 5355

Elephant House
21 George IV Bridge (0131) 220 5355
A shrine to those big footed grey fellows with great views of the castle. This cosy and slightly ramshackle café is a good place to escape the Royal Mile tourist trail for a quick regroup and refuel. Always busy, mostly due to its proximity to the uni, so you'll struggle to find a seat at peak times.
Mon-Fri 8am-11pm, Sat-Sun 9am-11pm

Elephants & Bagels
37 Marshall Street (0131) 668 4404
Little sister to the mighty Elephant House – not quite as hectic but equally as popular. Serves up a wide range of sweet, savoury and even breakfast bagels. Bagels are good for you, until, that is, you stuff them with the most calorific fillings you can lay your hands on, and eat five of them in a row.
Mon-Sun 8.30am-7pm

Filmhouse Café
88 Lothian Road (0131) 229 5932

Join the local film fanatics and brush up on your cinematic speak in this art house cinema café. A good place to whet your palate before you tuck into the latest anti-blockbuster offering or for a post-film, alcohol-fuelled debate.

Mon-Thu & Sun 10am-11.30pm
Fri-Sat 10am-12.30pm

Madly Mocha
43a Broughton Street (0131) 556 0085

A recent addition to Broughton Street, Madly Mocha makes seriously good coffee and a tasty selection of snacks to eat in or take away. Hearty meatballs to fuel you through the winter months and great salads for the summer, you won't be disappointed by this little caffeine haven. They also plan to extend the dinning area soon.

Mon-Fri 8am-3pm, Sat 9am-3pm
Closed on Sun

```
43b BROUGHTON STREET
EDINBURGH  EH1 3LX

T. 0131 556 0085
E. GOSSIP@MADLYMOCHA.CO.UK
W. WWW.MADLYMOCHA.CO.UK

TAKE-AWAY OR SIT IN AND RELAX
```

Starbucks
8-10 Bakers St (0131) 220 4908
Borders, Fort Kinnaird
Newcraighall Rd (0131) 657 9768
ESPC, 85 George St (0131) 624 8596
55 Forrest Road (0131) 220 5543
30A George St (0131) 220 5670,
106 George St (0131) 220 1451
Gyle Shopping Centre (0131) 229 4899
Ocean Terminal, Leith (0131) 554 4292
124 High St. The Royal Mile
(0131) 225 4201
Waterstone's, 128 Princes St
(0131) 226 3610

I'm afraid Edinburgh has been diagnosed with a nasty rash of corporate McCoffee houses. Clean, predictable, everywhere (actually, that's pretty handy), devoid of any character, but you can't argue with their Frappucinos. Still, there's something rather sinister about their sly domination of the city.

Mon-Sat 8.30am-7pm, Sun 10.30am-6pm

gay

www.itchyedinburgh.co.uk

The scene in Edinburgh centres around the fabled pink triangle of Leith Walk, but it's not hard to go out on a Friday night and move from bar to bar, only to find the same crowd have moved on with you. Pretty good if you're out on the hunt, but to avoid gay fatigue it's worth branching out to Broughton Street and Annandale Street. Most bars around the city are fairly gay friendly, especially those in Broughton Street, pre-club places like EH1 and ones attached to Theatres (like Traverse Bar). It's invariably male dominated but the bars included have a fair mix of women too.

Blue Moon Café

1 Barony Street (0131) 557 0911

More of a café than a bar, and a whole load more genteel than the rest of the places at the top of Leith Walk. Tucked away on Barony Street, it's the city's oldest gay café and pretty much ideal for that first date, if only so you can hear what your potential other half is saying rather than being drowned out by thumping techno. It's almost the sort of place you'd take the parents to show them good, wholesome gay folk, until they stroll downstairs to the toilet and find a sex shop instead.

Mon-Fri 11am-11.30pm
Sat-Sun 10am-11.30pm

Café Habana

Greenside Place (0131) 558 1270

Less sophisticated but no less fun than Planet Out, Café Habana has the bonus of a balcony from where you can pick out potentials to pounce on. It's also very brightly lit so you've only yourself to blame for any rude awakenings. Cheap drinks, Steps-orientated music and a good giggle.

Mon-Sat 12pm-1am, Sun 12.30pm-1am

CC Blooms

23-24 Greenside Place (0131) 556 9331

A mirrored monstrosity of a dancefloor and ear-bleeding techno in this old skool camp club filled with Edinburgh's slightly older gay aristocracy who still remember when it was great. Open every night, this is still a good laugh when you're battered and fancy some genuine kitsch. Oh, and avoid the dreadful wailing on Tuesdays when they have karaoke. For serious clubbing you'll still have to make your way over to Glasgow.

Mon-Sat 6pm-3am, Sun 8pm-3am

Laughing Duck
24 Howe Street (0131) 220 2376
This look-a-like All Bar One joint in the heart of New Town is the antidote to leopard print couches and lime green walls. It attracts a slightly older punter, rather than more hormonal types, and is chilled enough to actually hear what people are saying. A classy cut above the rest of the places here; Laughing Duck is pretty much the perfect place to start a night out.
Mon-Thu & Sun 12pm-12am
Fri-Sat 12pm-1am

Nexus Café Bar
60 Broughton Street (0131) 478 7069
Take refuge from the world of raging heterosexuals in this big, comfy living roomesque bar with massive windows that open up for the occasional Edinburgh sun, or simply to watch the rain whilst nursing a latté. Also worth checking out are the retro eighties arcade machines located just inside the entrance.
Mon-Sun 11am-11pm

Planet Out
6 Baxter's Place (0131) 524 0061
Planet Out remains the closest the Edinburgh gay scene gets to sophistication, and after a new lick of paint it's looking a lot fresher too. A young, well dressed crowd and lively late nights with Edinburgh's finest queers, plus they've got a load of extremely comfy sofas for when you just want to chill out and watch the totty. Especially worth a trip out for are the Pink Pound nights on Mondays (a pound to get in and all drinks are £1) and the quiz nights.
Mon-Fri 4pm-1am, Sat-Sun 2pm-1am

○ Club Nights

Taste
Every Sunday at the Liquid Rooms on Victoria Street, Taste is there for all of your house and garage needs.

Luvely
Hard House sweat session held monthly at the Liquid Room. First Saturday of every month.

Joy
Fortnightly Saturday night and about to go into its ninth year, Joy at Ego continues to pull in the punters. Pumping house upstairs and DJs (including Trendy Wendy) play a bit of everything, with a distinct whiff of cheese.

takno
An ever popular cheese-fest in the cosy confines of Club Mercado. A monthly Sunday event, so only for those with iron constitutions, an employment death wish or no job at all. Each event has a fancy dress theme which will get you in for less cash.

Vibe
Cheesy chart nonsense in this ever-sweaty weekly Tuesday night at Ego. Carefree, young, and jam-packed with glitter.

shopping
www.itchyedinburgh.co.uk

When to shop...
Generally Edinburgh shops are open as follows:
Mon-Wed 10am-6pm, Thu 10am-7pm
Fri-Sat 10am-6pm, Sun 12pm-5pm

○ Areas, Centres & Dept Stores

Cameron Toll Shopping Centre
Lady Road (0131) 666 2777
Give it a miss on the sartorial front but for all life's other necessities this place is the ticket. A massive Sainsbury's, car park, petrol station and all your high street essentials – Boots, Thorntons, BHS, you know the score. You won't be stuck for pants in here.
Mon-Sat 7.30am-10pm, Sun 8am-7pm

Frasers
145 Princes Street (0131) 225 2472
Frasers is the Selfridges/Harrods/Liberty's of the north with more designer clobber under one roof than the Beckhams could manage with a new extension. Come here for flash clothes and accessories in the kind of shopping environment that just cries out for an overdraft extension and a posh lunch.
Mon 9am-5.30pm, Tue 9.30am-5.30pm
Wed 9am-5.30pm, Thu 9am-7.30pm
Fri 9am-5.30pm, Sat 9am-6pm
Sun 9am-5.30pm

Gyle Shopping Centre
Gyle Avenue (0131) 539 9000

For high street shopping without the need to crowd surf through hordes of tourists and panic-stricken girls with a Saturday night date, head to the Gyle. It's a bit out of the way but perfect for one-stop retail missions and relishing the joy of a parking space.
Mon-Wed 9.30am-8pm, Thu 9.30am-9pm
Fri 9.30am-8pm, Sat 9am-6pm
Sun 10am-6pm

Harvey Nichols
30-34 St Andrew Square (0131) 524 8388

Edinburgh's sexy new Harvey Nic's has finally opened so, at last, you can live the Ab Fab lifestyle quaffing champers in the bar before heading through floors of clothes, cosmetics and fancy food. Pure, unadulterated and exclusively priced luxury.
Mon-Wed 10am-6pm, Thu 10am-8pm
Fri-Sat 10am-6pm, Sun 12pm-6pm

Jenners
47 Princes Street (0131) 225 2442

Pass me another scone, Elspeth. Let's talk handbags. The clientele of Edinburgh's Harrods-wannabe are a classy, tight-lipped and female bunch – something the department store's wares tend to reflect in taste and price range. Brandish a Jenners' bag, however, and your entry to any Morningside salon is assured. Poking through its labyrinthine and walnut-panelled interiors, you'll find designer labels a go-go with an emphasis on headscarves. The food hall is well worth exploring, especially for those with a taste in rare chutneys, and if you're visiting around Christmas, pop in and see the enormous tree.
Mon 9am-6pm, Tue 9.30am-6pm
Wed 9am-6pm, Thu 9am-7.30pm
Fri-Sat 9am-6pm, Sun 12pm-5pm

John Lewis
69 St James Centre (0131) 556 9121

Size matters in department store world and John Lewis isn't afraid to get naked in the showers. Ruling the roost of Edinburgh department stores, you'll find it stuffed full of pretty much everything you could and couldn't want.
Mon-Wed 9am-5.30pm, Thu 9am-7.30pm
Fri 9am-5.30pm, Sat 9am-6pm

Ocean Terminal
Ocean Drive, Leith (0131) 555 8888

The Ocean Terminal on Ocean Drive – unfortunately not as James Bond as it might sound. Instead of shaken martinis you'll find

a swanky new waterfront shopping centre next to the Royal yacht. Rather than Bond girls you'll find students and posh arty types tutting at the concept of a leisure park before browsing the high street brands.
Mon-Fri 10am-8pm, Sat 10am-7pm
Sun 11am-6pm

Princes Mall
Princes Street (next to Waverly Station) (0131) 557 3759
A few high street names, a surplus of tartan tourist traps and a food court... Princes Mall is not worth leaving Princes Street for, unless you're particularly desperate to pick up an Edinburgh Castle sun-visor.
Mon-Wed 8.30am-6.30pm, Thu 8.30am-7.30pm, Fri-Sat 8.30am-6.30pm, Sun 10.30am-5.30pm. NB: Shops close 1/2hour before Mall

St James Centre
Princes Street East (0131) 557 0050
Boasting one of the few car parks in central Edinburgh, the St James Centre contains the usual high street suspects: of particular note HMV and Topshop.
Mon-Wed 7.30am-6pm, Thu 7.30am-8.30pm Fri-Sat 7.30am-6pm, Sun 12pm-5.30pm

Cult Clothing Co.
7-9 North Bridge (0131) 556 5003
Cult is the daddy of all things hip. A favourite with both the clubbing and skating fraternity, it has become *the* place to shop with its range of unisex urban t-shirts, shirts, denims, trainers and bags.
Mon-Wed 9.30am-6pm, Thu 9.30am-7pm Fri-Sat 9.30am-6pm, Sun 12pm-5pm

Flip
60-62 South Bridge (0131) 556 4966
From original seventies denims and t-shirts to up-to-the-minute skate pants and zip-up track tops, Flip can sort out all your outfit needs in one easy go. If you'd rather not look like every other girl/boy down your local this place should be top of your list for something a bit original.
Mon-Wed 9.30am-5.30pm, Thu-Sat 9.30am-6pm

Freeze
Bruntsfield Place (0131) 228 2355
All the gear you need to look cool when you're out on the piste.
Mon-Sat 10am-6pm, Sun 12pm-5pm

Momentum
Bruntsfield (0131) 229 6665
Surf shop stocking the usual cool labels, this is the perfect place to pick up all your gear for a summer catching the waves on Bondi or... erm, Portobello beach.
Mon-Sat 10am-6pm, Sun 12pm-4pm

Shop 'til you drop

Odd One Out

16 Victoria Street (0131) 220 6400

OK, so we said previously that Cult is the daddy, but that all depends on who you are. It might be ok for the hoi polloi, but your flasher thinking urbanite shops here at Odd One Out. Rock up for labels like Lady Soul, Silas, Aei-Kei and Fly, as well as plenty of one offs and brands on sole distribution. No more looking like the masses for you...

Mon-Sun 10am-6pm

USC

97-98 Princes Street (0131) 220 2210

Urban, designer stuff for blokes who pick fights in nightclubs, and Meg Matthews (circa 1995) wannabes.

Mon-Wed 9am-6pm, Thu 9am-7pm
Fri-Sat 9am-6pm, Sun 11am-5pm

Xile

Princes Mall (0131) 556 6508

Designer gear centralis. Worth a detour from Princes Street, but keep your credit card limit topped up.

Mon-Wed 9am-6pm, Thu 9am-7pm
Fri-Sat 9am-6pm, Sun 11am-5pm

○ Women's Fashion

Coast

61 George Street (0131) 225 9190

Ok, so you've got the hot shot job, the gorgeous bloke and the swanky loft apartment – well you'd damned well better start looking the part before they discover you're a fraud. Kit yourself out here with flash clothes for girls at the top.

Mon-Wed 10am-6pm, Thu 10am-7pm
Fri-Sat 10am-6pm, Sun 12pm-5.30pm

Corniche

2 Jeffrey Street (0131) 556 3707

The ultimate in designer gear. You pay for the names (Westwood, Gaultier etc), but that's what it's all about... isn't it sweetie?

Mon-Sat 10am-5.30pm

Karen Millen

53 George Street (0131) 220 1589

Wedding outfits and bland, glittery office girl attire. Karen Millen has always been a bit above its station what with its fancy displays and designer prices. It really should know its place, but it doesn't.

Mon-Wed10am-6pm, Thu 10am-7pm
Fri-Sat 10am-6pm, Sun 12pm-5pm

Oasis
14-16 Frederick Street (0131) 225 4624

Stylish women's fashion with excellent in-house collections – Oasis offers clothes, shoes and accessories at affordable prices for your discerning girl about town. What more could a girl ask for? Umm, a hot date with Jude Law, holiday home on the French Riviera and Kylie's arse? They can't provide everything you know.
Mon-Wed & Sat 10am-6pm, Thu 10am-8pm
Fri 9.30am-6pm & Sun 12pm-5pm

Whistles
97 George Street (0131) 226 4398
Sophisticated, well-cut garments you'd happily sell all your internal organs to own.
Mon-Wed 10am-6pm, Thu 10am- 7.30pm
Fri 10-6pm, Sat 9am-6pm, Sun 12pm-5pm

○ Men's Fashion

Boardwise
4 Lady Lawson Street (0131) 229 5887
Boards galore and clothes to go with them – though don't go rocking up here banging on about sick waves in your O'Neill t-shirt.

This isn't a place for fashion victims – only proper sportsmen need apply.
Mon-Sat 10am-6pm

Corniche
12 Jeffrey Street (0131) 557 8333
Designer outfits for those who can afford them. Tragic window shopping or credit card debt for those who can't.
Mon-Sat 10am-5.30pm

Cruise
94 George Street (0131) 226 3524
14 St Mary's Street (0131) 556 2532
For the more discerning (read: richer) male shopper. Girls might want to hang out outside and see what they can pick up – they can't all be gay?
Mon-Wed 10am-6pm, Thu 10am-7pm
Fri 10am-6pm, Sat 9.30am-6pm
Sun 12pm-5pm

Geoffrey (Tailor) Kiltmakers
57-59 High Street (0131) 557 0256

Traditional Scottish and contemporary Highland dress to buy and hire for weddings, graduations and other embarrassing family occasions.
Mon-Wed 9am-5.30pm, Thu 9am-7pm
Fri-Sat 9am-5.30pm, Sun 10am-5pm

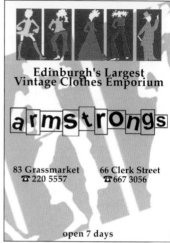

Edinburgh's Largest
Vintage Clothes Emporium

armstrongs

83 Grassmarket
☎ 220 5557

66 Clerk Street
☎ 667 3056

open 7 days

○ Secondhand

Armstrongs
83 The Grassmarket (0131) 220 5557
66 Clerk Street (0131) 667 3056
An experience not to be missed. You don't really count as an Edinburgh citizen until you've spent a day being transformed with-

in its hallowed walls. Here you'll find vintage and retro clothes as well as crazy stuff to cater for your every fancy dress whim. Far too easy to get carried away and spend the whole day transforming yourself into Marilyn Monroe – they do like it if you actually buy something.

Mon-Fri 10am-5.30pm, Sat 10am-6pm
Sun 12pm-6pm

Godiva
54 West Port (0131) 221 9212
Fashion scavenger heaven with racks of vintage clobber and plenty of handpicked hip stuff to save you rummaging through Kappa tracksuits all afternoon. Top notch.
Mon-Sat 12pm-6pm

Paddy Barass
Grassmarket (0131) 226 3087
Not just your average second hand emporium, Paddy's stocks vintage fabrics, lace and linen for a quite literally timeless look.
Mon-Fri 12pm-6pm, Sat 10.30am-5.30pm

Rusty Zip
14 Teviot Place (0131) 226 4634
A colourful fun-packed shop of potential, or a garish, headache inducing torture cham-

ber? It tends to depend on who's party you're being forced to attend next Saturday and how much of a total dick the resulting theme is going to make you look. Still, Rusty Zip is rammed with interesting attire – leathers, flares, flying suits, party wigs and 'taches galore.
Mon-Thu 10am-5.30pm, Fri-Sat 10am-6pm
Sun 12pm-6pm

YoYo
5 Clerk Street (0131) 622 7352
Colourful second hand gear ideal for fancy dress or perfecting your vintage-chic look.
Mon-Sat 11am-6pm, Sun 2pm-6pm

O Music

Avalanche
63 Cockburn Street (0131) 225 3939
28 Lady Lawson Street (0131) 228 1939
2-3 Teviot Place (0131) 226 7666
17 West Nicolson Street (0131) 668 2374
If you like your tunes loud and guitary you'll be happy browsing the indie, metal and rock offerings in here. Check out the bargain second hand CDs and have a break from the hordes in Fopp.
Mon-Sat 10.45am-6.15pm

www.itchyedinburgh.co.uk

WHATEVER TURNS YOU ON *Virgin* megastores

virgin.com/megastores

Fopp
55 Cockburn Street (0131) 220 0133

Fopp's 'suck it and see' policy sounds like a dodgy proposition. What it actually means is that if you decide Barry Manilow's Greatest Hits wasn't such a good acquisition after all, you can return your purchase with no questions asked. Maybe just a raised eyebrow. With the majority of CDs ranging from £5 to £10, vinyl downstairs and a selection of cheap books and videos, temptation is at a peak. Enjoy.

Mon-Sat 9.30am-7pm, Sun 11am-6pm

HMV
129-130 Princes Street (0131) 225 7008
43-44 St James Centre (0131) 556 1236

Great sales, a massive range and an equally massive shop. Every music, DVD and video need catered for with finesse.

Pr. St: Mon-Wed, Thu 9am-8pm
Fri-Sat 9am-6pm, Sun 11am-5.30pm
St J: Mon-Wed 9am-6pm, Thu 9am-7.30pm
Fri-Sat 9am-6pm, Sun 11.30am-5pm

Hog's Head Music
63 South Clerk Street (0131) 667 5274

Essential student shop specialising in secondhand music on all formats along with DVDs, videos and a range of new but grungy t-shirts.

Mon-Sat 10am-5.30pm, Sun 1pm-5pm

Professor Plastics Vinyl Frontier
15a West Richmond St (0131) 622 7168

Hardcore rare vinyl for fanatics. Professor Plastic offers up quality LPs you never realised you liked or wanted until you crossed the threshold. This place comes highly respected and recommended.

Mon-Sun 11am-6pm

Ripping Records
91 South Bridge (0131) 226 7010

One of the main ticket outlets in town supplying gig tickets for most major concerts, festivals and club nights in Edinburgh and Glasgow. They also do a good line in mainstream music and budget CDs.

Mon-Wed 9.30am-6.30pm
Thu 9.30am-7pm, Fri-Sat 9.30am-6.30pm
Sun 12pm-5pm

Underground Solu'shun

9 Cockburn Street (0131) 226 2242

A good specialist dance shop well-stocked with everything from techno to hip hop, as well as virtually any sub-genre you can think of. Vinyl makes up the majority of the stock but you will also find CDs, videos, hardware, record bags, t-shirts and spray paint for all your vandalism needs.

Mon-Wed 10am-6pm, Thu 10am-7pm
Fri-Sat 10am-6pm, Sun 1pm-5pm

Vinyl Villians

5 Elm Row, Leith Walk (0131) 558 1170

Specialising in those little black discs with an impressive secondhand stock. Music rummagers will lose hours and spend hard in here.

Mon-Sat 7.15am-6pm, Sun 12pm-4pm

Virgin

124 Princes Street (0131) 220 2230

Singles, albums, videos, games and general music-biz accessories from one of our favourite big time music retailers.

Mon-Wed 9am-6pm, Thu 9am-8pm
Fri-Sat 9am-6pm, Sun 11am-6pm

O Books

Beyond Words

42-44 Cockburn Street (0131) 226 6636

In the midst of arty Cockburn Street this unique shop offers an excellent array of photography books. You'll find practical guides, criticism and photojournalism, as well as books on cinema, music, wildlife and landscape. Interesting gifts are well catered for here too.

Mon 12pm-5pm, Tue-Sat 10am-6pm
Sun 12pm-5pm

Borders

Fort Kinnaird, Newcraighall Rd
(0131) 657 4041

Books galore with a cosy 'feel free to flick' kind of feel. The coffee shop and evening classes/gatherings are worth checking out and you'll find the biggest selection of magazines in Edinburgh. Particularly impressive is the lesbian and gay selection.

Mon-Sat 9am-10pm, Sun 11am-8pm

James Thin

53-59 South Bridge (0131) 556 6743
29 Buccleuch Street (0131) 667 6253

University booksellers with a mammoth classic literature section and just about every textbook you could possibly wish didn't exist.

Mon 9am-9pm, Tue 9.30am-9pm, Wed-Fri 9am-9pm, Sat 9am-5.30pm, Sun 11am-5pm

Waterstone's

13-14 Princes Street (0131) 556 3034
128 Princes Street (0131) 226 2666
83 George Street (0131) 225 3436
The original revamped bookstore has been revamped yet again. Whether you like the clean modern instant access look they've given the ground floor of the George Street branch is your decision entirely. We reckon it does the job but we still can't get enough of the old school Princes Street branch for a bit of literary browsing.
Mon-Fri 9am-8pm, Sat 9am-7.30pm
Sun 10am-7pm

WHSmiths

Haymarket Station (0131) 346 4531
10b Queensferry Street (0131) 225 9672
Waverley Station (0131) 557 1175
Books, stationery and the like. You'll have to head out of the city to find the bigger outlets.
Mon-Sun 7am-6pm NB. Hours vary between stores so call to check.

Word Power

43 West Nicolson Street (0131) 662 9112
Just round the corner from Edinburgh University, Word Power is a tiny, independent bookshop that corners the alternative market. Push past the wind-chimes beneath the door and you'll come upon a treasure trove of feminist and radical fact and fiction, plus some moderately subversive postcards. Staff are happy to order in anything you can't find, and to advise if you're unsure about what you're after. They also love it when you start abusing their views and declaring it all a load of airy, fairy, flaky rubbish – honest.
Mon-Sat 10am-6pm

O Other cool shops

Aha Ha Ha

99 West Bow (0131) 220 5252
88 Grassmarket (0131) 225 3388
Every six year old boys dream shop – we're talking fake dog turds and fart cushions galore. And, if you've mislaid you're gorilla suit you'll find you can borrow one from their costume hire department no problem.
Mon-Sat 10am-6pm, Sun 12pm-4pm

Crabtree & Evelyn

4 Hanover Street (0131) 226 2478
It's Christmas, your auntie's birthday, mother's day or maybe your girlfriend's in a mild huff... gifts for girls and a few things for boys to boot. C & E is pricey and luxurious. Note however, that although this stuff is perfect for ageing female relatives, your bird is only

going to be impressed if she's cool enough to appreciate its retro appeal. If she reads Cosmo and likes the Corrs stick with something from Boots.
Mon-Wed 10am-6pm, Thu 10am-7pm Fri-Sat 10am-6pm, Sun 12pm-5pm

Crystal Clear
52 Cockburn Street (0131) 226 7888
Hokey bohemian crystals and books on wicca, yoga and ancient mysticism. Full of girls who've just been dumped by their boyfriends convincing themselves that a bit of rose quartz will get him back from that tart from the video shop.
Mon-Sun 9.30am-6pm

The Finishing Touch
17 St Patrick Square (0131) 667 0914
All your beading and cake-decorating needs met in one confused store. We find it hard to believe too but people honestly do keep telling us how they can't live without this place. Not all our reviewers are insane – we hope.

Foam Centre
176 Causewayside (0131) 668 4508
This shop sells foam, padding and bean-bag fillings. Which just about puts paid to the claim earlier regarding reviewer sanity. A

dubious inclusion for this year's shopping section – but it's got comedy value.
Mon-Sat 9.30am-5.30pm

Forbidden Planet
40-41 South Bridge (0131) 558 8226
Edinburgh's sci-fi paradise. If you want the new edition of your favourite comic (Batman, not Beano), the follow up merchandise, Buffy posters or the latest Simpson or Star Wars toy then this is your shop. Your geek alert should be on maximum.
Mon-Sat 10am-5.30pm, Sun 12pm-5pm

Ground Control
33 Cockburn Street (0131) 622 7317

Get pierced, get tattooed, get your hands on some baggy jeans, band t-shirts and enough smoking paraphernalia to have the place teaming with teenage boys from open to close. Not a bad option if you're a teenage girl on the pull.
Mon 9.30am-6pm, Sun 12pm-5pm

Halibut & Herring
108 Bruntsfield Place (0131) 229 2669
31 Raeburn Place (0131) 332 5687
89 West Bow (0131) 226 7472
Yes, you really do need that inflatable bath pillow with goldfish on it, you know, to

match the shower curtain and bath mat you bought here last week.
Mon-Sat 10am-6pm, Sun 11am-5pm

Paper Tiger
53 Lothian Road (0131) 228 2790
16 Stafford Street (0131) 226 2390

Here you will find the perfect stocking filler no matter what time of year – a particularly popular purchase being the postcard book of 70s male models wearing knitted pants. Your high street card shop this is not, so be prepared to pay over the odds for your goodies.
Mon-Sat 9.30am-6pm
Stafford St: Also Sun 11am-5pm

Remnant Kings East
88 Newington Road (0131) 667 7210
43-45 Lothian Road (0131) 229 5135
The Newington branch is perfect for last minute costumes and amateur dress-making with friendly staff to boot. Lothian Road is more hardcore upholstery focused.
Mon-Sat 9am-5.30pm, Sun 12pm-5pm

Space NK
103 George Street (0131) 225 6371
Lotions and potions to make you more beautiful than you already are. Pricey.
Mon-Wed 10am-6pm, Thu 10am-7.30pm
Fri-Sat 10am-6pm

entertainment & culture
www.itchyedinburgh.co.uk

○ Festivals

Edinburgh Fringe Festival
180 High Street (0131) 226 0026

Who in their right mind would plan to hold five festivals at the same time? A: Edinburgh. Every August Edinburgh swells to gargantuan numbers and, while the purists come solely for the Festival, the majority of people descend upon Auld Reekie for the world famous Fringe festival. Set over three weeks, in over a hundred venues, more than 600 companies will stage over 1,500 shows that could be anything from stand up comedy to surreal sitcom, French mime to expressionist dance. If it all sounds a bit manic then that's because it is. The Fringe is one of the biggest events of its kind and is suitably loud and brash. It can be very hit or miss, but that's part of the appeal.
August

International Book Festival
137 Dundee Street (0131) 228 5444

For the more literary of you out there the Edinburgh International Book Festival offers a rare opportunity to hear the writers you love and revere speak. For the extremely highbrow there's the opportunity to pose intellec-

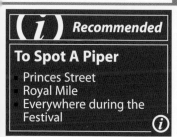

(*i*) Recommended

To Spot A Piper

- Princes Street
- Royal Mile
- Everywhere during the Festival

tual and deep-delving questions to the authors, such as, does being a writer guarantee lots of sex? And for any budding Rushdies there's the chance to engage in workshops to fine-tune your own writing skills.

August

International Festival
The Hub, Royal Mile (0131) 473 2000

The original and oldest Edinburgh festival has been well and truly ousted from centre-stage by the limelight-hogging Fringe. All the same, if it's high culture you're after then this is the festival for you. Showcasing global theatre, opera, dance and music for those who prefer a more traditional approach to the arts.

August

International Film Festival
88 Lothian Road (0131) 229 2550

It may lack the glitz and glamour of Cannes and the grittiness of Sundance, but the World's oldest film festival still manages to combine the exotic with the blockbusting to bring together nearly a month's worth of cinema, talks and workshops from around the globe. Given the diversity of the festival, it's possible to experience things like live director's commentaries, premiers of next year's

Oscar nominees and weird Bolivian art house cinema within a matter of hours – an extreme sensory experience if nothing else. The down to earth nature of the screenings also means that you could have a slightly dazed Frank Skinner trying to sit in your mate's seat, or end up kicking the back of Vinnie Jones' (not a good idea). Being as high profile as it is, and completely open to the public, tickets for the big screenings go really quickly, so get your applications in early.

August

International Jazz & Blues Festival
29 St Stephen Street (0131) 467 5200

For hardcore jazz and blues fans or for those who fancy trying something a bit different. Prices vary but it's worth keeping an eye out for the freebies in Princes Street Gardens.

August

Military Tattoo
32 Market Street (0131) 225 1188

Screened on TVs across the world, the Tattoo is staged in the grounds of Edinburgh Castle. With bagpipes and kilts galore, the tourists can't get enough of it. Book early because it will sell out.

August

Beltane

An annual pagan fertility fest takes Calton hill by storm on May Day, when a bunch of crusties dance around in various states of undress to the beat of many drums... If it sounds like your idea of hell, then it probably is. Likewise if it sounds like your idea of a great night out, it probably is. There are no in-betweens when it comes to pagan festivals.
1st May

Hogmanay

This is bigger than Christmas. Edinburgh really has got New Year down to a fine art. Every year Hogmanay takes Scotland's capital by the throat, force-feeds it half the population of Britain, and several million crates of bubbly, before instigating a rousing chorus of Auld Lang Syne. If you don't enjoy crowds then you may as well forget it as there's hardly any room to swing a very small gerbil. If that doesn't sound like your cup of tea, then bugger off back to where you came from.
31st December... obviously

○ Places to visit

Arthur's Seat

If you're looking for a natural wonder, then this 350 million year old extinct volcano can't be beaten. Providing spectacular views of the city, it's a tradition on the last night of Freshers' Week for students to wrap warm, take plenty of booze (and any other stimulants they can get their grubby little hands on) and scale the rocky heights to watch the sunrise on a lifetime of debt. Expect plenty of fresh air, hernia-inducing exercise, and brisk winds that can blow you off the peak faster than you can say the word 'lemming'.

Calton Hill

Another scenic spot, but far easier to climb than that sodding volcano, and home to Edinburgh's disgrace. This is the best place

to watch the Hogmanay and end of Festival fireworks. It really comes into its own on May Day when hundreds of crusties congregate to celebarate Beltane and the birth of the new year in traditional psychotropic pagan fashion. The rest of the year sees some rather x-rated goings on involving lots of men.

Cockburn Street

Branching off from the tourist infested Royal Mile, this winding street features a number of independent retailers and coffee shops frequented by the terminally hip. Music and

vinyl junkies will drool over the criminally cheap bargains to be found in Fopp and Avalanche. You'll find most things you need, and a few things you don't on this street.

Edinburgh Castle

Precariously perched on yet another bit of volcano, this is Scotland's most popular and immaculately maintained tourist attraction. Within its walls are housed the Scottish Crown Jewels, the Stone of Scone, and various other national treasures. Freshers should steer well clear as superstition dictates that those who visit before the end of

their first year will be cursed never to graduate. Just don't be a muppet and ask what time they fire the One O' Clock Gun.
Open: 9.30am-6pm 1st April-31st October, 9.30am-5pm 1st November- 31st March
Entry: Adults £7.50, Children £2

The Edinburgh Dungeon
31 Market Street (0131) 240 1000

A fascinating, and sometimes nerve-wracking voyage through how punishment was meted out to wrongdoers in years gone by. You get to see in vivid detail the numerous methods of punishment that our forefathers had to endure for even the most petty of crimes. The hung, drawn and quartered method, which was handed out to those people who really stepped out of line, is a particular favourite exhibit of ours, but we at itchy had to shiver when we saw that forgery was punishable by the loss of a hand. All in all a great day out, just so long as you're not a total wuss.
Nov-Mar: Mon-Fri 11am-4pm, Sat-Sun 10.30am-4.30pm, Apr-Jun: Mon-Sun 10am-5pm, Jul-Aug: Mon-Sun 10am-7pm, Sep-Oct: Mon-Sun 10am-5pm.
Adult £8.50, Child/OAP £5.50, NUS £6.50

George Street

Playground of Edinburgh's fabulously wealthy, but not necessarily beautiful, people. Chock-full of flash bars, fine restaurants and expensive stores for all your designer needs. A great place if you want to show off to all your less well endowed acquaintances, or, if you're like me, the first stop on your way to round up those pretentious tossers for the firing squad come the revolution. Only joking, in no way whatsoever would we at itchy promote the raising of arms and taking of life of the bourgeoisie all in the name of a peoples' revolution. You can leave that sort of malarkey to the French.

Ghost Tours
The Tron, Hunter Square

Edinburgh has more underground goings-on than Venice has canals and there's a huge variety of tours designed to appeal to your spirit of adventure. You'll find them guided by jobbing actors in make-up provided by Dulux and armed with rubber rats and second-hand tales. Entertaining and sometimes even scary (if you're stoned enough).

Greyfriar's Bobby
George IV Bridge, Candlemakers Row

According to legend, a Skye terrier named Bobby was so devastated by its master's death in 1858 that he took up residence at his graveside in Greyfriar's kirkyard, thus cunningly avoiding the extortionate rental prices of getting a proper home. The dog was cared for by the sympathetic patrons of the nearby pub, which takes his name, until his death fourteen years later. This statue was erected as a testament to Bobby's loyalty, and a symbol to all naughty pups everywhere. Check out the saccharine 1950s film in glorious technicolour and "authentic Scotch" cast.

Palace of Holyrood
Canongate, Royal Mile (0131) 556 7371

Situated at the bottom of the Mile this working palace has a fascinating bloody past. David Rizzio, Mary Queen of Scots' secretary and lover had his throat slit from ear to ear (talk about giving head) in one of its many lavish apartments. Open all year round except when in use by her Royal Queenness.
Open: 9.30am-6pm, April-October, 9.30am-4.30pm, November-March
Entry: £6.50 Adults, £5 Senior Citizens, £3.30 Children, £16.50 Family ticket

Princes Street

Edinburgh's main street and the dividing line between the Old and New Towns. A mixture of beautiful Georgian and horrendous 1950s and 60s architecture on the north side this bustling shoppers delight features all the usual high street names. The south side is flanked by the beautiful Princes Street Gardens (once a grubby marshy loch), Waverly Station, two excellent galleries, Edinburgh Castle and the Gothic phallus that is the Scott monument

Royal Yacht Brittania
Ocean Drive, Leith (0131) 555 5566

Way down deep in the Port of Leith lies the final resting place of Her Majesty's Coracle Britannia. The Royals never seem to tire of charging the public to visit their ridiculously extravagant old residences, which takes the piss seeing as we paid for them in the first place. Your once in a lifetime opportunity to snoop around the private rooms of the Queen and her old silky tongued codger of a husband, the Duke of Edinburgh.
Open: 9.30am-4.30pm, tours every 15 mins
Entry: £7.75 Adults, £3.75 Children, Family ticket £20

Rose Street

This cobbled little lane is jam-packed with pubs, cafes, pubs, shops and pubs. If you're looking for pubs, you've definitely come to the right place, and if you think you're 'ard enuff you can have a go at the Rose Street Pub Crawl. The goal is to have a pint in each pub and make it from one end of the street to the other, but if you puke you have to go back and start all over again. Scots never puke though, so if you see someone being sick they're probably English.

Royal Mile

This is an integral part of life in the capital stretching from the Castle Esplanade at the top, to Holyrood Palace down at the bottom. In between you'll find ancient tenement buildings, and shops selling huge varieties of whisky, kilts, haggis and a whole host of other cultural delights and pure kitsch. You'll also find the Fringe Office, The Scotch Whisky Heritage Centre, St. Giles Cathedral, the City Chambers, John Knox House and various museums. Street parades and parties are scattered across the year. All in all this is one fine stretch of road.

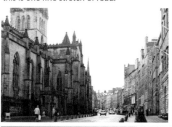

Scottish Whisky Heritage Centre

354 Castlehill, Royal Mile (0131) 220 044

The complete and unabridged history of th national drink, presented in an entertainin and tacky manner with a fifteen minute ric in a barrel (yes, a barrel) through a series 'dramatic scenes'. At the end of which you' presented with a free dram, and once you' learned the fundamentals of alcohol distill tion you can then go home and start expe imenting with your own lethal brand homebrewed moonshine.
Open: 9.30am-5.30pm 7 days a week
Entry: £6.50 Adults, £2.75 Children

Scott Monument

East Princes St Gardens (0131) 529 4068
Built in honour of Scotland's greatest nove ist, Sir Walter Scott. If you're up to it you ca climb up several flights of gradually narrow ing stairway to witness an amazing and ve tigo inducing view over Edinburgh.
Open: 9am-7pm Mon-Sat, 10am-6pm Sun
Entry: £2.50

The best seats out of the house

○ Live music & theatre

Assembly Rooms
George Street (0131) 226 2428
Predominantly a comedy and theatre venue, this place really comes into its own during the Edinburgh and Fringe Festivals, when the line-up is usually the hottest in town.

Edinburgh Corn Exchange
11 Newmarket Road (0131) 477 3500
Opened by Blur in 1999, since when the likes of Pulp, Coldplay, David Gray and Travis have trod the boards. As have Toploader, but hopefully they won't allow such a crime to occur again.

Edinburgh Playhouse
18-22 Greenside Place (0131) 557 2692
A 3000 capacity venue which puts on concerts from artists as diverse as Badly Drawn Boy, Liberty X and Def Leppard as well as theatre, children's shows and musicals.

Festival Theatre
13-29 Nicholson Street (0131) 529 6000
A big glass-fronted theatre that houses the biggest stage in Britain. It's so big that even

Rik Waller would have room to breakdance, not that you'd be likely to see many head-spins inside here as it's predominantly opera and ballet productions on show. Other events include musicals and children's shows. Very cultured.

King's Theatre
2 Leven Street (0131) 529 6000
If you're after a bit of diversity without having to endure the over-acting of people who should have retired from the stage after 6th form college then the King's Theatre is the place to come. They hold visits from the Royal National Theatre and other major touring productions, as well as Edinburgh's annual pantomime.

Royal Lyceum Theatre
30 Grindlay Street (0131) 248 4848

This beautiful Victorian theatre has for many years now been the best place in Scotland to view leading productions of contemporary and classic theatre. The Royal Lyceum Theatre Company produces eight plays a

Get out more in the all-new Ford**Fiesta**

year, and they have a policy of encouraging guest directors, designers and lighting designers to generate fresh ideas. Ideally situated amongst numerous pubs, bars, restaurants and cinemas so you can drink like a barbarian and redeem yourself with a slice of culture.

Queens Hall
Clerk Street (0131) 668 3456

Renowned as being one of the best jazz venues in the UK, and home to the Scottish Chamber Orchestra. You can also catch classical, blues, pop, rock, world, folk and comedy events. There's a bar inside which is worth a visit alone to sample the real ales – if you like real ales that is.

Traverse Theatre
10 Cambridge Street (0131) 228 1404

Dedicated to the production and development of new Scottish writing, some of which have won awards, some of which are embarrassingly bad. The theatre also hosts performed readings, workshops, special events and writers groups. The best bit is the bar downstairs which serves some very decent tapas. A portion of patatas bravas or some obscure experimental theatre – you decide.

Usher Hall
Lothian Road (0131) 228 8616

Mightily impressive venue which provides a home to the Royal Scottish National Orchestra. If that's not your bag then you can also catch a number of bands who have usually past their best such as Sinead O'Connor and those denim-wearing hell raisers Status Quo.

○ Comedy

Assembly Rooms
George Street (0131) 226 2428

The list of comedians who've performed at the Assembly Rooms reads like a who's who of the UK comedy scene. Performers have included Frank Skinner, Lee Evans, Mark Lamarr and Peter Kay to name but a handful. During the Fringe Festival you can be certain to catch some quality acts, but you'll have to book well in advance because it gets stupidly busy at that time of year.

The Stand Comedy Club
5 York Place (0131) 558 7272

The first specialised comedy venue in Edinburgh and still the best place to go and see established acts as well as those who are on the way up (or about to go rapidly down hill). Performance prices range from free, for the highly entertaining improv sets on Sunday lunchtimes, to £8 on Saturday nights. If you haven't already, then we strongly recommend that you rock up for a night at The Stand, but just make sure you book in advance because this venue is as busy as a plumber with lots of plumbing to do. *Check www.itchyedinburgh.co.uk for regular listings updates*

O Internet access

Comms Port @ Costa Coffee

35 Shandwick Place (0131) 228 6322
1 Hanover Street (0131) 228 5868
Housed in Costa Coffee so you can grab a cappuccino whilst you wait for a terminal to come free.
Mon-Sat 8am-8pm, Sun 10am-7pm
(Shandwick St) Mon-Sat 8am-7pm, Sun
10am-6pm (Hanover St)

easyEverything

58 Rose Street

High-speed connections at low prices. This is literally the easiest place to get online as there's more than enough screens to go round. There's a wide variety of food available and plenty of room to spread out.
Mon-Sun 7am-11pm, Access starts from £1

Web13

13 Bread Street (0131) 229 8883
Internet access as well as printing, faxing and photocopying. They serve some great food to chew on whilst you clear your Hotmail account of numerous porn links and people trying to sell cheap insurance.
Mon 10am-8pm, Tue-Sat 10am-10pm
Sun 12pm-6pm, Access £1 per 20mins

O American football

Scottish Claymores
Murrayfield (0131) 478 7200
Surprisingly popular here in Auld Reekie. With all the American-style, pre-match trimmings this is sport with an emphasis on showmanship.

O Basketball

Edinburgh Rocks
**Meadowbank Sports Centre
(0131) 661 5351**
Tall men throwing balls through hoops.

O Football

Heart Of Midlothian F.C.
Tynecastle, Gorgie Road (0131) 200 7200
If you're looking for silky passing football and £50k a week primadonnas with one eye on the ball and the other on their next sponsorship deal then it's safe to say this isn't the team for you. Tynecastle is for those who yearn for afternoons spent sipping Bovril and trying to prevent the grease from their Scotch Pies dripping onto their jeans. Best games to watch (for atmosphere as opposed to quality) are against Hibs, Celtic and Rangers.

Hibernian F.C.
Easter Road (0131) 661 1875

Hibs have yet to reach a league position to match up to the refurbished stadium and its swanky function rooms (containing the biggest chandeliers in Scotland, I'll have you know), but there is a feeling in the Leith air that new manager Bobby Williamson may be able to come up with the goods, not winning the championship of course, but a good cup run would be very welcome. And, whilst there aren't any real superstars on the pitch, there are plenty of celebs in the stands – Irvine Welsh, Dougray Scott and pals have stayed loyal to their team no matter what the results.

O Ice hockey

Edinburgh Capitals
Murrayfield Ice Rink (0131) 313 2977
Legalised violence on ice. They've changed their name more times than Prince. Fast, furious and fun for all the family

Edinburgh Gunners
Meadowbank Stadium (0131) 661 5351
Another year of getting gubbed by every other team in Europe awaits.

O Rugby Union

Murrayfield
West Maitland Street (0131) 346 5000

Going to see a Scotland v England match at Murrayfield should be on everyone's list of the 10 things they must do before they die. This is the only truly world class stadium in Scotland, and one to feel proud of.

O Karting/laser/paintball

Karting
Raceland (0131) 665 6525

Let's face it, all males like the idea of fast cars and competition. Far better than driving around in a white Escort listening to shitty hardcore music.

12pm-10.30pm all week
Adults: £15 for two 10 minute sessions
Children: £6 for 10 minutes

Laser Quest
3 Bread Street (0131) 221 0000

Have your machismo annihilated and suffer abject humiliation at the hands of pre-pubescent kids playing hookie from school.

11am-11pm Mon-Sat, 11am-8pm Sun
Off peak (11am-6pm Mon-Fri) £3.50
On peak (every other time) £4

Bedlam Paintball
28 Great King Street (0131) 558 1919

Indulge your violent fantasies by gunning down your boss in a hail of pellets. Not as bloody but definitely as messy. Disgustingly satisfying as you get in touch with your inner Arnie. Alternatively, you could walk around in sandals, insisting that war is not the answer and pleading for people to put down their guns, then you can pop a cap in their asses

3 Sessions. Morning: 9am, Afternoon: 1pm, Evening: 5pm
Prices: £20, £40, and £50 (depending on the number of pellets). All equipment provided

O Bowling

Megabowl
Fountain Park, Dundee Street
(0131) 478 9999 or 478 3000
5 Kinnaird Park (0131) 657 3731

If chucking huge mighty balls at a load of skittles is your cup of tea then this is the place for you – you can even do it in the dark. Booze and food aplenty.

Open 'til 12am Sun-Thu, 2am Fri & Sat

O Out of Edinburgh

Firth of Forth

Bus No. X5 to Gullane leaves from St Andrew Square.

On either bank of the Forth you'll find a selection of lovely and not-so-lovely beaches. Gullane is just far enough out of the city to feel remote (i.e. squint and you can't see a powerstation) but still on the bus route. If you're feeling a little bit more adventurous head over to Fife on the train for some coastal scenery and views back across the waters to Auld Reekie.

Glasgow

Glasgow Tourist Info 08705 992 244

Less than an hour away by train is the land of Buckfast and perpetual rain. Nah, it's not that bad really. Over the past few years Glasgow has received regular cultural injections and it's on a definite high. Throw into the bargain an abundance of bars and restaurants and a selection of shops that are guaranteed to send you into a spending frenzy. Enticed? You should be. Overwhelmed? Pick up a copy of itchy Glasgow 2003 for the good, bad, where's and what's of Scotland's funkiest city.

GoByCoach.com

[The place to go for cheap travel]

Go by coach... Leeds
Cost: £35.50 economy return
Time taken: From 6 hours 30 mins
Journeys: 2 each way

So, sum it up then...
Self-proclaimed UK 2nd city... vibrant... diverse feel...

Eating out...
Fuji Hiro (45 Wade Lane [0113] 243 9184) is the best bargain noodle bar in town. For something more fancy try Calls Grill (38 The Calls [0113] 245 3870) or Livebait (The Calls [0113] 244 4144).

Slake that thirst in style...
We rate the North Bar (24 New Briggate [0113] 242 4540) and Norman's (36 Call Lane [0113] 234 3988). The whole of Call Lane is worth checking out.

Not ready for bed yet...
Try the Mint Club (8 Harrison St [0113] 244 3168) for an intimate clubbing vibe or Elbow Rooms (64 Call Lane [0113] 245 7011) for late night DJs and pool.

What about daylight hours?
Roundhay Park is well worth a look (check out tropical world for two quid) or try some Victorian Quarter shopping.

And when the party's over...
The Crescent Hotel (274 Dewsbury Rd [0113] 270 1819) should do the job for cheap B&B.

NATIONAL EXPRESS »

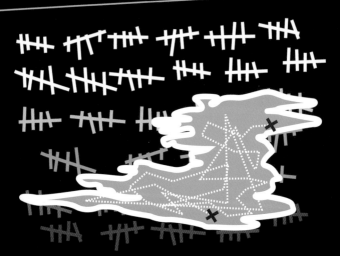

Glenkinchie Distillery
Pencaitland (01875) 342 004

One of the few monuments to Scotland's favourite tipple in the Edinburgh area. Surprisingly not as mundane as it sounds as you get a detailed history of the spirit – but no mention of the fact that almost all of us have been horrendously sick at some point after drinking too much of the stuff. For hardcore whisky fanatics or for those of you who just want the free taster at the end, Glenkinchie is well worth a look.

St Andrews
**Kingdom of Fife Tourist Board
(01592) 750 066**

A mecca for golf lovers everywhere, during the Open St Andrews is full to bursting with Americans in Pringle sweaters and the occasional celebrity (well, golf loving celebrities at least). For those of you who wouldn't know a golf club from a cricket bat, there's always the option of a bit of Royal-spotting since Oor Wullie headed north of the border to become the UK's most famous student.

O Culture

As the cradle of Western civilisation as we know it (sorry to puncture all your Yank and Sassenach delusions), where Adam Smith, David Hume and William Robertson plied their various trades, we canny Scots have more culture sloshing around than whisky and Bucky. So take your time, wander around and be educated like you've never been educated before. Or you could just jump in the nearest boozer.

O Museums and galleries

The Dean Gallery
**73 Belford Road (0131) 624 6200
Recorded info (0131) 332 2266**

Opened in 1999 and situated just opposite the Modern Art Gallery with a superb collection of works on display.

10am-5pm Mon-Sat, 12pm-5pm Sun
Free entry, although some exhibitions may have a charge.

The Fruitmarket Gallery
45 Market Street (0131) 225 2383

Designed by one of Edinburgh's top architects, this small yet perfectly formed gallery plays host to a variety of contemporary art exhibitions. And just in case you're wondering what's the point of it all, they kindly provide a bookshop with everything you need to know and a café to mull it over in.
11am-6pm Mon-Sat, 12pm-5pm Sun
Free entry, although some exhibitions may have a charge

Museum of Childhood
42 High Street (0131) 529 4142
Be amazed at what kids got up to before the invention of the PlayStation. Laugh and be embarrassed as you watch your parents regress back to snotty, grubby little five year olds. And be eternally thankful that you never had any of these given to you for Christmas presents.
10am-5pm Mon-Sat.
Occasionally open on summer Sunday afternoons.
Free entry

Museum of Scotland
Chambers Street (0131) 225 7534
A quite stunning addition to Edinburgh's architectural and cultural landscape. Attached to the rambling Royal Museum (so you can kill two birds with one stone) this is a top class museum in which Scotland's history is presented on seven levels from the Prehistoric to the present and everything else in between.
Mon-Sun 10pm-5pm (Tue open 'til 8pm)
Free entry

National Gallery of Scotland
The Mound (0131) 624 6200

As if to prove to anyone south of the border that London is not the cultural centre of the universe, the humble (alright, maybe not that humble) National Gallery has pulled off a number of coups in last few years including the first showings of the highly successful Rembrandt and Monet exhibitions.
10am-5pm Mon-Sat, 12pm-5pm Sun
Free entry, although some exhibitions may have a charge.

Royal Museum of Scotland
Chambers Street (0131) 247 4219

A museum like a museum ought to be. An eclectic collection of natural history, engineering, Arabic and Eastern Art and just about everything else you could think of. The Ivy Wu Gallery on the top floor is worth the visit alone with its spectacular collection of Chinese, Japanese and Korean artefacts.
10am-5pm Mon-Sat (8pm on Tue)
12pm-5pm Sun Free entry

Scottish National Gallery of Modern Art
Belford Road (0131) 624 6200
Set in some delightful gardens that features a number of the exhibits. Ideal for a walk round with your parents in an attempt to convince them that you really aren't a drunken moron. Or it's good to walk off that hangover whilst feeling mildly intellectual as you do it. All in all it does exactly what it says on the door.
10am-5pm Mon-Sat, 12pm-5pm Sun
Free entry, although some exhibitions may have a charge.

Scottish National Portrait Gallery
1 Queen Street (0131) 624 6200
(Recorded Info. 332 2266)
Full of big pictures of big people (and some small ones) who are now fertiliser. They also do a tasty line in cakes at the café.
10am-5pm Mon-Sat, 12pm-5pm Sun
Free entry

Stills Gallery
23 Cockburn Street (0131) 622 6200

A cool, vibrant little gallery that tries its hand at a bit of everything. You're not likely to get anything like the National Gallery experience, but then that's the whole point.
10am-5pm Tue-Sat
Free entry

Unit Photographic
166 High Street (0131) 220 1044
This is where you get to show off and buy something a little bit special. A contemporary photographic gallery showing the work of some of Edinburgh's finest upstart photographers.
Fri-Sat 11am-5pm or by appointment

Useful Numbers
Body
Accommodation
Entertainment
Takeaway

useful info
www.itchyedinburgh.co.uk

O Useful Numbers

Taxis & Private Hire
Airport Taxis	(0131) 344 3344
Area Cabs	(0131) 448 0009
Bee Dee	(0131) 663 8541
Cabtime	(0131) 220 3444
Capital Castle	(0131) 228 2555
Central Radio Taxis	(0131) 229 2468
City Cabs	(0131) 228 1211
Festival City	(0131) 552 1777
Pentland Taxis	(0131) 440 2525
Premier Cars	(0131) 660 1031
Raeburn	(0131) 315 3333

Or buy your own. Try www.getoutmore.com

Bus Companies
City Link	08705 50 50 50
First Edinburgh	(0131) 663 9233
Lothian	(0131) 555 6363
National Express	08705 80 80 80
Stagecoach	(0141) 552 4961

Train Companies
National Rail Enquiries	08457 48 49 50
Virgin Trains	0870 789 1234

Airports
Edinburgh Airport	(0131) 333 1000
Glasgow Airport	(0141) 887 1111
Prestwick Airport	(01292) 479 822

Tourist Info
3 Princes Street	(0131) 473 3838

Useful Info
British Gas (Emergency)	0800 111 999
Childline	0800 11 11 11
City Council	(0131) 200 2000
City Hospital	(0131) 536 6000

Dyno-locks (24hr locksmiths)	**NHS Direct** 0845 4647
....0800 316 4602	**Rape & Abuse Line**.................0808 8000 123
Edinburgh Royal Infirmary	**RSPCA** 0870 5555 999
....(0131) 536 1000	**Samaritans** 08457 909 090

body

○ Hairdressers

Sleek blonde highlights, a nifty new Mohawk or just a last minute short back and sides before a Friday night on the town...

Medusa
26 Bread Street (0131) 622 7277
6-7 Teviot Place (0131) 225 6627
22 High St, Musselburgh (0131) 665 1199
Guaranteed to grab the object of your affection's attention without turning them to stone - they didn't make it to the finals of the British Hairdressing Awards for no good reason, you know. Top notch cuts and colours with an entire floor dedicated to the art of colour at Teviot Place , a private beauty area at the Musselburgh branch and individual booths generally housing a celeb or two at Bread Street.

For opening times and prices see table

Name	Address	Pricing	Hours
Hairdressers – men			
Bailey's Barbers	39 Clerk Street (0131) 477 2905	£6	Mon-Sat 9am-6pm, (Thu-Fri 'til 7pm)
Hairdressers – women & unisex			
Charlie Miller	39 Frederick Street (0131) 225 1141	Women £19.50-£45, Men £19.50-£36	Mon-Wed & Fri 9am-5.30pm, Thu 10am-6.30pm,Sat 8.30am-5pm
Charlie Miller	13 Stafford Street (0131) 226 5550	Women £27-£45 Men £28.50-£36	Mon-Wed & Fri 9am-5pm,Thu 9am-6pm, Sat 8.30am-4.30pm

Name	Address	Pricing	Hours
Charlie Miller	8 South St Andrew St (0131) 556 9898	Women £19.50-£45, Men £25.50-£36	Mon-Fri 9am-5.30pm (Thu 9am-6.30pm), Sat 8.30am-5pm
Cheynes	77 Lothian Road (0131) 228 9977 45a York Place (0131) 558 1010 57 South Bridge (0131) 556 0108 46 George Street (0131) 220 0777	Women £23/£31/£36, Men £20.50/£26/£31	Mon-Fri 9am-6pm (Thu 9am-7.30pm), Sat 9am-4.30pm
Medusa	26 Bread Street (0131) 622 7277 6-7 Teviot Place (0131) 225 6627 22 High St, Musselburgh 665 1199	Women £24/£30/£34.50, Men £19.50/£24.50/£28 ('til 8pm at Teviot Place, 'til 7.30pm at Musselburgh),	Mon-Wed & Fri 9am-6pm, Thu 9am-8.30pm Sat 9am-4.30pm
Mosko	17 North Bridge (0131) 557 6968	Women from £24.50, Men from £14.50	Mon-Thu 9am-9pm, Fri 9am-8pm, Sat 9am-5pm, Sun 10am-5pm
Munro Macleans	Rose Street (0131) 226 3576	Women from £28.50, Men from £20.50	Mon-Fri 9.30am-6pm (Thu 'til 7pm), Sat 9am-4pm
Patersons	129 Lothian Road (0131) 228 5252	Men & Women £25/£30/£35	Mon-Fri 9am-6pm, Sat 9am-4.30pm
Patersons	60 George Street (0131) 226 3121	Men & Women £30/£35/£40	Mon-Fri 9am-6pm, (Thu 10.30am-7.30pm) Sat 9am-4.30pm
Toni & Guy	141 George Street (0131) 220 5425	Women £33/£39/£45 Men £26/£29/£45	Mon-Wed 9am-6pm, Thu 10am-8pm, Fri-Sat 9am-6pm
All times and prices correct at time of going to press			

○ Beauty/Gyms/Tans/Tattoos

Beauty is only skin deep so you'd better make the most of what nature has given you. Thankfully there are heaps of places to help you improve your lot - try some of these for size. Whether you're looking for a waxing, a workout, a healthy golden glow or full blown body art, you'll find it here. Why wait for special occasions?

Name	Address	Pricing	Hours
Beauty Salons			
Celeste Spa	1a Leven Street (0131) 221 1900	Facials from £30	Mon-Fri 9am-8pm, Sat 9am-6pm, Closed Sun
Notes: Waxing, manicures, pedicures, facials, non-surgical facelifts, day spa treatments			

GoByCoach.com

[The place to go for cheap travel]

efore deciding how you're going to travel check out our low fares, they're
eriously good value, and, they're available when you want them. If you're
ged between 16-25 or a student save even more on travel with a Young
ersons' Discount Coachcard. Cards cost £9 and give you up to 30% off already
ow fares all year. GoByCoach.com provides the easiest way to book last minute
ravel - Simply book your journey, print off your e-ticket and show it to the
river when you board. Register online to receive news of special offers and
nd out how you can spend and earn with GoByCoach points.

Coach services depart from St Andrew's Square, South Side, Edinburgh

Check online for details.

Study Hard..

Play Hard...

Relax!

Memberships from as little as just £8 per week for students & ITCHY readers PLUS £100 off the joining fee on production of this advert! Facilities include state-of-the-art gymnasia, luxury swimming pools, over 50 exercise classes per week, kid's club... and much more!*

HOLMES PLACE
one life. live it well

CALL YOUR NEAREST CLUB NOW TO SEE IF YOU QUALIFY FOR
VIP DAY PASS FOR YOU & A FRIEND!**

StarCity, Birmingham
0121-322-8700

Nottingham
0115-988-4747

Parrswood, Manchester
0161-249-5600

Printworks, Manchester
0161-831-9922

Edinburgh (new c
0131-550-1650

* Facilities vary between clubs   ** Conditions apply, for a full list of clubs - check out the website below!
www.holmesplace.com

Name	Address	Pricing	Hours
Essential Therapy	49 Broughton Street (0131) 557 8444	Facials £15-£30	Mon & Fri 9.30am-5.30pm, Tue-Thu 9.30am-7.30pm, Sat 9.30am-3.30pm

Notes: Beauty therapy services. Closed Sun.

| Zen Lifestyle | 9 Bruntsfield Place (0131) 477 3535 | Facials from £40 | Mon-Fri 8am-10pm, Sat 9am-6pm, Sun 10am-6pm |

Notes: Massage, manicures, pedicures, facials, reflexology, electrolysis

Health Clubs & Gyms

Name	Address	Pricing	Hours
Bannatyne's Health Club	43 Queen Street (0131) 225 8384	Call for prices	Mon-Fri 6.30am-10pm, Sat-Sun 8am-8pm

Notes: 25m pool, aerobics studio, 2 gyms, members lounge, sauna, sun beds, steam room, spa,

| Edge Health and Fitness | Lochside Place, Edinburgh Park (0131) 339 0181 | Joining fee £35, £45.90 per month | Mon-Fri 7am-10.30pm, Sat-Sun 8am-8pm |

Notes: Gym, fitness studios, pool, spa, sauna, steam room, hair salon

| Fitness First | 30 Abercrombie Pl. (0131) 558 7887 | Approx. £35/month | Mon-Fri 6.30am-10pm, Sat 8am-9pm, Sun 8am-10pm |

Notes: Gym, 'cardio theatre' (with choice of 16 music/TV channels), exercise studio, video library, lounge bar, sauna, steam room, spa, sun beds, beauty salon

| Holmes Place | Opens Jan 2003 | | Call for prices (see opposite for special deals for **itchy** readers) |
| Living Well | Caledonian Hilton Hotel, Princes Street (0131) 222 8836 | Call for prices | Mon-Fri 6.30am-9.30pm, Sat-Sun 7am-8pm |

Notes: Gym, pool, beauty salon, solarium, aerobics, sauna, steam room, spa, café/bar

| The Gym | 2-12 Marionville Rd | Off peak £19/month, Peak £24.50. No joining fee. | Mon-Fri 9am-9pm, Sat-Sun 10am-4pm |

Notes: Pool, gym, sun beds

| Reviva | 59 Bread St (0131) 228 8990 | £65 joining fee Call for rates. | Mon-Fri 9am-9pm, Sat-Sun 10am-5pm |

Notes: Women only. Gym, toning tables, dance studio with 31+ classes, computerised resistance machines.

Tanning Studios

Name	Address	Pricing	Hours
California Tan	St Stephen St (0131) 220 2045	Standing: £2 for 3 mins, £3.50 for 6, £5 for 9.	Mon-Fri 9am-8.30pm, Sat-Sun 'til 7.30pm

Notes: With membership the £7.50 session is only £5. Membership costs £10 a month/£20 for 3

| Hi-Tech Tanning Studio | 100 Marchmont Rd (0131) 447 7411 | £2 for 6 mins, £1 for every 3 mins after | Mon-Fri 9am-11pm, Sat 9am-6pm, Sun 11am-11pm |

Tattoo Parlours

Name	Address	Pricing	Hours
Blue Tiger Tattoo	343 Easter Road (0131) 555 0009	Prices vary	Mon-Sat 11am-6pm, Closed Sun
Bizarre Ink	9 East Fountainbridge (0131) 221 0677	Prices vary	Mon-Sat 9am-6pm, Sun 10am-6pm
Tribal Body Art	248 Canongate (0131) 558 9019	Prices vary	Mon-Sat 11am-6pm, Closed Sun

accommodation

Expensive: Looking for somewhere to stay where they're going to worry about the important things in life like the thread count of the sheets in your hotel? Look no further...

Mid-Range: Not one for extremes then are we? Nothing too posh, nothing too skanky - just somewhere that suits that inbetween.

Budget: For those weekends away when drinking, shopping and clubbing have to take priority over silk bathrobes

Name	Address	Price w/day	Price w/end	Notes
Expensive				
Argyll Town House	Rothesay Place (0131) 622 6800	£100	£100	Four Star. Inc. full Scottish b'fast
Bank Hotel	1 South Bridge (0131) 622 6800	£110	£110	Rooms celebrate famous Scots. Inc. full Scottish b'fast
Balmoral Hotel	1 Princes St (0131) 556 2414	£210+	£210+	Breakfast not included
Caledonian Hilton	Princes St (0131) 222 8888	£210+	£210+	–
Channings	12/16 South Learmonth Gardens (0131) 315 2226	£170+	£170+	Inc. full Scottish b'fast.
Crowne Plaza	80 High St (0131) 557 9797	£99+	£99+	–
George Intercont.	19-21 George St (0131) 225 1251	Rack rate £205	Rack rate £205	Breakfast not included.
Malmaison	1 Tower Place (0131) 468 5000	£120+	£120+	–
Menzies Belford	69 Belford Rd (0131) 332 2545	£99+	£99+	Inc. full Scottish b'fast.
Park Hotel	4 Alvanley Terr. (0131) 622 6800	£90	£90	Inc. full Scottish b'fast
Point Hotel	34-36 Bread St (0131) 221 5555	£105	£105	–
Rothesay Hotel	8 Rothesay Place (0131) 622 6800	£90	£90	Two star. Inc. full Scottish b'fast
Royal Ettrick Hotel	13 Ettrick Rd (0131) 622 6800	£90	£90	Three star. Inc. full Scottish b'fast.
Tailors Hall Hotel	139 Cowgate (0131) 622 6801	£110	£110	Cobbled c/yard & beer garden. 3 Sisters pub next to the reception. Inc. full Scottish b'fast.
Mid-range				
A-Haven Town	180 Ferry Rd (0131) 554 6559	£30+	£30+	Inc. full Scottish b'fast
Ailsa Craig Hotel	24 Royal Terrace (0131) 556 1022	£25+	£25+	Inc. full Scottish b'fast

Name	Address	Price w/day	Price w/end	Notes
Ballantrae Hotel	8 York Place (0131) 478 4748	£70+	£70+	Inc. full Scottish b'fast
Holiday Inn	Britannia Way, Ocean Drive, Leith 0870 744 2163/555 4422	£62+	£62+	Inc. continental b'fast.
Ibis	Hunter Square (0131) 240 7000	£45+	£45+	Breakfast an additional £4.95
Navaar House	12 Mayfield Gdns (0131) 667 2828	£60+	£60+	Inc. full Scottish b'fast
Osborne Hotel	53-59 York Place (0131) 556 5577	£84+	£84+	Inc. full Scottish b'fast
Raeburn House	112 Raeburn Pl. (0131) 622 6800	£55	£55	Inc. full Scottish b'fast
Tailors Hall Hotel	139 Cowgate (0131) 622 6801	£75+	£75+	Inc. full Scottish b'fast
Budget				
Brodie's Backpackers Hostel	12 High St, Royal Mile (0131) 556 6770	Mon-Thu £9.90+	Fri-Sun £11.90+	Dorms only. No b/fast.
Castle Rock Hostel	15 Johnston Ter. (0131) 225 9666	£11+	£11+	Single sex dorms. No breakfast.
Edinburgh Backpackers Hostel	65 Cockburn St (0131) 220 1717	£12.50+	£12.50+	Dorms only. No breakfast
Princes St East Backpackers	5 W. Register St (0131) 556 6894	£11+	£11+	Dorms only. No breakfast
Princes St West	3 Queensferry St (0131) 226 2939	£12 (winter), £16 (summer)		Dorms only. No breakfast

entertainment

So you've sworn off the evil liquor, you've exhausted every possible option in the realms of home entertainment, from plasma screen TVs to power drilling, and now all you want is some good old fashioned fun. From big screen movie action to gambling away your life savings, it's all right here...

Name	Address	Pricing	Hours
Mainstream Cinemas			
Odeon	7 Clerk St 0870 505 0007	Adults £4-£5.30 Conc. £3.20	Daily 12pm-last showing (Sun-Thu 9pm ish, Fri-Sat 11pm ish)
Ster Century	Victoria Dock, Leith Docks (0131) 553 0700	Adults £4.50-£5.50, Kids/OAPs £3, NUS £3.50	Daily 10am last showing (9.30pm ish)
UCI	Kinnaird Park, Newcraighall Rd 08700 102 030	Adult £4.25-£5.25, Kids/OAPs £3.65, NUS £3.95	Daily 11am-10pm (ish)
UGC	Fountain Park 0870 902 0417	Adults £4.20+£5.20 Kids £3, NUS/OAP/UB40 £3.20	Daily 11am-last showing (Sun-Thu 9.30pm ish, Fri-Sat 11pm ish)

Name	Address	Pricing	Hours
Snooker/Pool			
The Angle Club	3 Jordan Lane, Morningside (0131) 447 8814	£1 entry for non-members. Snooker from £4.50 per hr, pool from £6.	Daily 10.30am-12am (Tue opens at 12pm, Sat closes at 1am)
The Angle Club	25 Jocks Lodge (0131) 661 4323	Details as above	Sun-Fri 11am-12am, Sat 10am-12am
Diane's Pool Hall	242 Morrison St (0131) 467 7470	20p per game	Daily 8am-1am
Strip Joints			
Fantasy Bar	16 Home St (0131) 221 9030	Entry £10 (inc. 1 dance). Additional dances £5 each.	Sun-Fri 4pm-1am, Sat 12pm-1am
The Western Bar	157-159 W.Port (0131) 229 7983	Entry: Mon-Thu free b4 9pm, £3 after, Fri-Sat £4 all day. £5/dance.	Mon-Wed 1pm-12am, Thu-Sat 1pm-1am, Sun 2pm-7pm
Bowling/Karting/Paintball/Casino's etc			
Bedlam Paintball	28 Great King St (0131) 558 1919	From £20	Daily 9am, 1pm & 6pm (Summer only)
Ed. Capitals Ice Hockey	Murrayfield Ice Rink, Riversdale Crescent (0131) 313 2977	Adults £9, Conc. £5	Most Sun nights Sep-Mar, 6pm-8.30pm
Laser Quest	56b Dalry Rd (0131) 346 1919	£4 for 1 game, £7 for two, £9 for three	Mon-Sat 11am-11pm, Sun 11am-8pm
Megabowl	5 Kinnaird Park (0131) 657 3731	Adult £3.75, Kids £2.75, NUS £1.50 per game. Shoe hire £1	Sun-Thu 10am-12am, Fri-Sat 10am-2am
Megabowl	Fountain Park, Dundee St (0131) 478 9999	Adults £4.95/game Kids £3.95	Mon-Thu 12pm-12am, Fri 12pm-2am, Sat 10am-2am, Sun 10am-12am
Midlothian Ski C/tre	Hillend (0131) 445 4433	Call for details	Summer: Mon-Fri 9.30am-9pm, Sun 9.30am-7pm. Call for winter hours.
Raceland	Tranent, East Lothian (0131) 665 6525	Adults 20 mins £25 Kids 20 mins £10 (indoor only)	Call for times. Booking essential.
Stanley Casino	2 Rutland Place (0131) 228 4446	Free. 24hr registration	Sun-Fri 2pm-6am, Sat 2pm-4am
Stanley Ed. Casino	5b York Place (0131) 624 2121	Free. 24hr registration	Sun-Fri 2pm-6am, Sat 2pm-4am

takeaway

If you're looking at this sober good luck to you...In a round up of the city's takeaway options you have to take the rough with the smooth. The top notch fish'n'chips with the dodgy kebabs. There's a fast food option for all but the fussiest inebriated diner here. Some of the establishments listed opposite are best approached when very, very drunk. You have been warned.

medusa® www.medusahair.co.uk

Name	Address	Delivery	Hours
Pizzas & Burgers			
Burger King	Princes Street (0131) 557 9128	No	Mon-Sat 6.30am-12am, Sun 8am-12am
Central	15-16 Teviot Place (0131) 226 6898	Yes	Sun-Thu 11.30am-1.45pm/
			4.30pm-1.30am (Fri-Sat 'til 3am)
Domino's Pizza	101 Nicolson Street (0131) 667 8666	Yes	Mon-Thu 12pm-12am,
	166 St Johns Road (0131) 334 6600		Fri-Sat 12pm-1am, Sun 12pm-11pm
King Kebab House	24 Albert Street (0131) 553 7859	Yes	Sun-Thu 12pm-2pm/4pm-12am
			(Fri-Sat 'til 1am)
Mamma's	30 Grassmarket (0131) 225 6464	Yes (after 5/6pm)	Mon-Fri 10am-11pm,
			Sat-Sun 10am-12pm
Mamma's	1 Howard Street (0131) 558 7177	Yes (after 5/6pm)	Mon-Fri 12pm-11pm,
			Sat-Sun 12am-1am
McDonald's	3 South St Andrew St (0131) 5589348	No	Sun-Thu 7am-12pm, Fri-Sat 7am-2am
McDonald's	137 Princes Street (0131) 226 3872	No	Sun-Thu 7am-12pm, Fri-Sat 7am-2am
No.1 Kebab	222 Morrison Street (0131) 538 5050	Yes	Daily 5pm-1am
Perfect Pizza	12 South Clerk Street (0131) 668 4599	Yes	Mon-Fri 4pm-12am, Sat-Sun 12pm-12am
Pizza Paradise	34 George IV Bridge (0131) 226 6706	No	4pm-3am
Indian & Asian			
Babas Indian T/way	261 Dalry Road (0131) 346 1015	Yes	Sun-Thu 5pm-12am, Fri-Sat 5pm-1am
Bangalore	52 Home Street (0131) 229 1348	Yes	Sun-Thu 5pm-12am, Fri-Sat 5pm-1am
Lasani	44 South Clerk Street (0131) 667 0239	Yes	Mon-Thu 12pm-3pm/5pm-12am
			Fri 12pm-3pm/5pm-2am
			Sat 5pm-2am, Sun 5pm-12am
Oriental			
Dragon Way	74 South Clerk St (0131) 668 2323/	Yes (after 5pm)	Mon-Sat 12pm-2pm/
	(0131) 662 8484		Sun 5pm-11pm
GY Chinese Takeout	26 Roseneath Place (0131) 229 9922	Yes	Sun-Mon 5pm 'til late
Palace			
Fish & Chips			
Clamshell Fish Bar	148 High Street (0131) 225 4338	Yes	Sun-Thu 11am-12.30am,
			(Fri-Sat 'til 2am)
Eatalia's	1 Brunswick Place (0131) 557 8484	Yes	Mon-Sat 11.30am-2pm/4.30pm-1am
			Sun 4.30pm-1am
Other			
Baked Potato Shop	56 Cockburn Street (0131) 225 7572	No	Daily 9am-9pm
Mex2Go	56 South Clerk Street (0131) 622 6266	Yes ('til 10.30pm)	Sun-Mon 5pm-11pm
Subway Sandwich	43 Hanover Street (0131) 226 4333	No	Mon-Thu 9am-9pm, Fri-Sat 9am-3am
	11 Forrest Road (0131) 220 0889	No	Mon-Fri 10am-11pm, Sun 11am-9pm

This section does not apply to new Ford Fiesta drivers

laters

www.itchyedinburgh.co.uk

O Late-night drinking

Blessed with probably the most endearing licensing laws in Britain, Edinburgh boasts a bevvy of bars that stay open 'til the wee small hours. **Berlin Bierhaus** and **Medina** stay open 'til 3am, as does **Po Na Na** (although they charge a couple of quid later in the week). Those of you with a severe case of insomnia, **The Penny Black** opens its doors at 5am (and, no, that's not a typo).

O Cigarettes at 4am?

Got the munchies? You're going to need an all night petrol station then. The best of the bunch are **Windmill Service Station**, 109 Queensferry Road and **Canonmills Service Station**, 23 Canonmills. Both are open 24 hours a day, seven days a week.

O After-hours fridge stocking

Peckham's on Raeburn Place and Bruntsfield Place is the place to stock up in style. Upmarket deli produce to tempt the finickiest of eaters as well as the all-important liquor to wash it all down with. Both branches are open Monday to Saturday from 8am 'til midnight and 9am 'til 11pm on Sundays. For those of you who find bran flakes too heavy on the stomach you can grab some alcohol instead from 9am Monday to Saturday (12pm on Sundays).

⭕ Food now!

Sometimes only instant nourishment is going to fit the bill and you're unlikely to find finer quality pizzas than those from **Pizza Paradise** on South Bridge, open 7 days a week from 4pm-3am. Or get into some Stateside **Subway** action on Hanover Street, on Friday and Saturday nights they're open 'til 3am.

⭕ Café society

Come over all continental and catch up with friends over a late night cappuccino. **Beanscene** on Holyrood Road and Nicolson Street is open seven days a week 'til 10pm. Views of the nearby castle add to the atmosphere at **Café Lucano** (open Monday-Saturday 'til 10pm) and **Elephant House** (open seven days a week 'til 11pm). They're both on George IV Bridge.

⭕ Late-night shopping

The majority of shops in Edinburgh stay open 'til 7pm on Thursdays. **Gyle Shopping Centre** is open 'til 8pm Monday-Wednesday and Fridays and 9pm on Thursdays. **Harvey Nichols,** meanwhile, is open 'til 8pm on Thursdays, whilst **Ocean Terminal** is open 'til 8pm Monday-Friday and 7pm on a Saturday.

⭕ After-work beauty fix

Are deadlines and office politics taking their toll? Rejuvenate mind and body at **Celeste** 'til 8pm. Or seek refuge at **Zen**, they'll soothe stressed out souls 'til 10pm. And for that year-round glow, where better to turn the perfect shade of caramel than **Hi-Tech Tanning Studio** on Marchmont Road, they're open Sunday to Friday 'til 11pm.

⭕ Late-night culture

Not strictly cultural, but if it's French and on late then it's as cultural as we're gonna get in the midnight hour. The **Cameo Cinema's** midnight movie fits the bill perfectly and guarantees you won't have to wade through the pre-schoolers crowd.

⭕ Other

Throughout the evening **Ghost & Ghouls Tours** leave from the Royal Mile and are perfect for a bit of cheesy, touristy and at times downright scary entertainment. If surfing the information highway's more your bag then **Easy Everything** on Rose Street fits the bill perfectly – they're open seven days a week from 7am 'til 11pm. Or simply indulge in some pool action at **Diane's Pool Hall** on Morrison Street.

⭕ Steer clear after dark

A far cry from downtown LA in the danger stakes, Edinburgh is pretty safe as long as you don't act like an arse – if you're English try to avoid speaking loudly (or at all) unless you've always dreamt of waking up in casualty. If you're on your own it's best to give the **Meadows** a wide berth as, like all secluded parks, it's a mugger's paradise. The **Cowgate** is also best avoided unless you enjoy the company of inebriated Edinburgh folk.

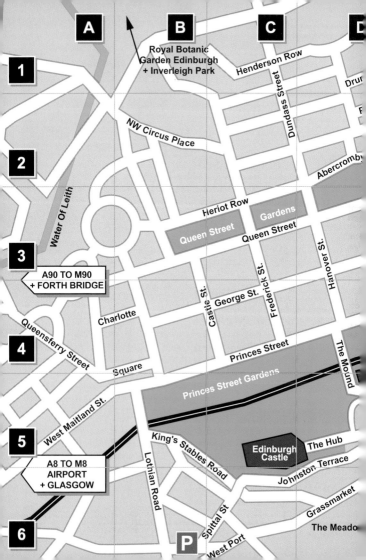

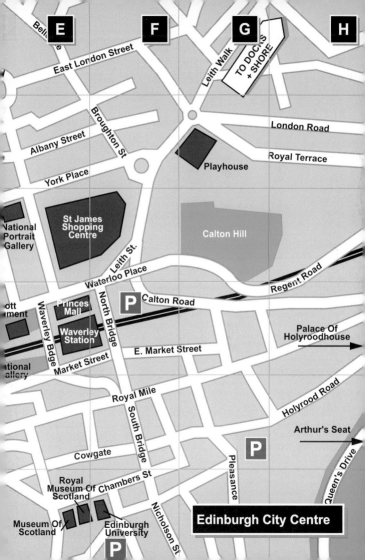

index

Fun-loving couple seeks adventure.
Finds it. The End.